A Little Thing I Tied Myself

Stories of Atlantic Canadian Fly Tiers

Don MacLean

NIMBUS
PUBLISHING

Nimbus Publishing Limited
PO Box 9166
Halifax, NS B3K 5M8
(902) 455-4286

Printed and bound in Canada

Design: James Somers
Author photo: Jason LeBlanc

Library and Archives Canada Cataloguing in Publication

    MacLean, Don, 1954-
    A little thing I tied myself : stories of
    Atlantic Canadian Fly Tiers / Don MacLean.

Includes bibliographical references and index.
ISBN 1-55109-537-8

1. Fly tyers—Atlantic Provinces. 2. Fly tying—History. 3. Flies,
Artificial. 4. Fly fishing—Atlantic Provinces. I. Title.

SH571.M25 2006 799.12'4'09715 C2006-900694-6

We acknowledge the financial support of the Government of Canada through the Book Publishing Industry Development Program (BPIDP) and the Canada Council, and of the Province of Nova Scotia through the Department of Tourism, Culture and Heritage for our publishing activities.

Acknowledgements

This book would not have been possible without the help of a great many people. My deepest appreciation is extended to the fly tiers and their families for allowing me to interview them and for graciously providing flies and photographs. My special thanks go out to the following people for their assistance with the writing of this book: Eric Baylis, Bill and Brenda Carpan, Bill Ensor, Dave and Bertha Fram, Bryant Freeman, Dewey Gillespie, Fred Harrigan, John Hart, Dick Huggard, Ches Loughlin, Rick Maddigan, Joanne Mailman, Katherine Mott, Keith Piercey, Bernie Price, Lennie and Monique Vassallo and Frank Walsh. I also want to thank Sandra McIntyre, Heather Bryan and all the staff at Nimbus Publishing for giving me the opportunity to write this book and for helping to make it a reality.

This book is dedicated to my wife Judy. Without her love, help and support, it would not have been possible.

Table of Contents

Preface: Which Fly to Use?
The Age-old Question

"I approach the subject of flies with the certainty that no opinions, experiences or views on the matter can be advanced which will not run counter to those of many masters. I have never met two reasonable anglers who would not differ radically as to some of their doctrines regarding flies."

Dean Sage
Salmon and Trout *(1904)*

It was late June on Nova Scotia's St. Mary's River as I waded through Harrison's Pool, hoping that the high water after a heavy rain two days before might bring in the first run of grilse. Several other anglers were already fishing there, and as the morning wore on we rotated through the pool without success. I was new to salmon fishing, and spent half the time thinking that there weren't any salmon in the river and the rest of the time convinced that I didn't have the right fly tied to the end of my leader.

Halfway through the pool on my third pass, I heard a splash and looked up to see an angler at the head of the run playing a grilse. It was obviously not his first salmon; he bowed to every jump and snubbed each run. He soon slid the fish up on the shore. We gathered around to congratulate him and admire the grilse. It was bright silver, and several sea lice dotted its flanks, a sure sign that it had just run in from the sea. Lacking the tact of the more experienced anglers in the group, I asked, "What did you catch him on?" Grinning, the old angler replied, "Oh, a little thing I tied myself." Gathering up his gear, he headed back to the car.

When I began salmon fishing many of the old-time anglers were a secretive bunch, and anglers had to go to great lengths to find out which flies had caught fish. Over time, as I paid my dues through several unsuccessful years on the river, I gained their confidence. Out of both pity and friendship they gradually opened up their fly boxes, and I seldom left the river without a new pattern. Most of these flies were simple drab patterns, and their success could mainly be attributed to the anglers' skill in presenting them.

Waldo Hendsbee's Five Cent Fly is a good example of the simple and effective fly patterns developed by Atlantic Canadian fly tiers. They reflect the demands of local fishing conditions and the innovative spirit of the fly tiers, who would turn to the farmyard and forest for their materials. Natural deer hair, feathers from the barnyard rooster, wool yarn, cotton thread, shoe makers' wax and varnish for head cement have all found their way into these old-time salmon flies. Tinsel for bodies was non-existent; fly tiers cut the tops of tobacco tins or toothpaste tubes into thin strips.

When I was conducting research for an article on the late Joe Aucoin, a well-known Cape Breton fly tier, I had the opportunity to interview Rick MacDonald. As a boy Rick had fished with Aucoin and was familiar with his flies. We talked about Aucoin's salmon patterns, the Brown, Black and Silver Gray Bombers, the Mystery and the Ross Special, and Rick told me that except for the Ross Special, Joe's flies are gone off the river. Rick's comments stayed with me and they planted a seed that would eventually take root and form this book.

The tradition of tying simple, sparse patterns is alive and well, as evidenced by the flies contributed to this book by amateur and professional fly tiers throughout Atlantic Canada. I have attempted to provide a snapshot of Atlantic Canadian fly tiers, past and present, who have developed, and continue to develop, fly patterns for use on the waters of Atlantic Canada. While the early tradition of fly tying is closely connected to patterns for Atlantic salmon and trout, today's tiers are also developing new patterns for species such as shad, small-mouth or striped bass and chain pickerel.

There are many fine fly tiers, both past and present, not covered in this book. For the definitive work on New Brunswick fly tiers I would direct readers to Dewey Gillespie's book, *Where the Rivers Meet: The Fly Tyers of New Brunswick*, which was privately published in 1995. Unfortunately, it is out of print. However, Dewey has recently developed a website, www.nbflytyers.com, which provides excellent profiles of New Brunswick fly tiers. I would refer those interested in the fly-tying history of Newfoundland and Labrador to Don Hutchens's articles in *SPAWNER* magazine.

I have not included any reference to tying details such as hook style, size, and head colour, except as mentioned by the tier. With the wide variety of hook styles available from a variety of makers, almost all the flies included in the book could be tied on any style of hook. While in most cases black is used as the head colour, occasionally, as in the Cosseboom, other colours are specified. Hook size is also dependent on a variety of factors ranging from water levels and season of the year to time of day and weather conditions. In the tradition of Atlantic Canadian fly tying, I have left it to the individual fly tier to use whatever material he or she has on hand. If this book introduces a new fly tier to the lore, innovation and wisdom of fly tiers of Atlantic Canada, writing it will have been time well spent.

Fly Tying in Atlantic Canada: A Short History

"If a fly is neat and workmanlike, well-shaped, and with wing and hackle dressed sufficiently lightly to play freely in the water, it is of comparatively small importance what pattern or of what colors the various parts are composed."

A. H. Chaytor, Letters to a Salmon Fisher's Sons *(1910)*

When the first Europeans arrived in Atlantic Canada they found rivers full of trout and Atlantic salmon, a bounty that helped fuel future exploration and settlement. This abundant resource was already well known to First Nations peoples, who depended on fresh- and salt-water fish for survival. Once, on the Gander River, our guide pointed out the remains of a fishing weir used by the Beothuks to capture salmon. To the untrained eye it looked like a line of rocks in the river, but using it, Beothuk fishers could direct large fish such as salmon and trout into a narrow area where they could be speared. Another fish-harvesting method involved the weaving together of branches against the framework of rocks and the funnelling of fish into a box trap. In the Maritimes, Mi'kmaq and Malecite harvesters used similar methods to capture not only salmon and trout but also shad, gaspereau, striped bass and eels.

The first European settlers were not anglers. Sport fishing was not a popular activity; few people had the free time required to participate, especially when fish could be easily caught with net or spear. Angling in Atlantic Canada had its development as a diversion for the wealthy. According to Charles Hallock, who wrote on sport fishing during the mid-1800s, "Fly fishing was in its infancy then. It was an act scarcely known in America and but little practiced in England." One of the earliest references to sport fishing in Atlantic Canada is attributed to the eighteenth-century English naturalist Joseph Banks. In August of 1766, Banks was on the *Niger*, a British ship sent to Newfoundland to protect Britain's fishing interests. Banks was on the voyage to investigate the natural history in Newfoundland and Labrador. He said this about the colony's fishing potential:

So much for salt water fish—the Fresh are in great Plenty tho but of 2 sorts, Trout and Eels, the first of which offered good Diversion to an angler biting Very well at the artificial, Particularly if it has gold about it, with this Peculiarity: in the rivers they are to be caught in abundance no where but in the tide and at no time but from about two hours before high water till Ebb in Pools. Indeed they always bite but best in sunshining weather. I have seen no large ones—none I believe above half a Pound in weight—but am told that in some Parts of Nfland they are Very Large.

From this description it sounds like the first sport fishing in North America was for sea run brook trout. Although his reference to an "artificial" does not specifically refer to a fly, flies would have been the most probable kind of lures used at that time. Noted angling historian Paul Schullery suggests that Banks' account is the first written reference to fly fishing in North America.

While the first written mentions of fly fishing in Atlantic Canada may have been in reference to trout fishing, most of the early literature refers to flies, and fly fishing, for Atlantic salmon. This can be attributed to the backgrounds of the region's first anglers, many of whom were British military officers stationed in garrisons in New Brunswick or Nova Scotia. They had gained their angling experience on the rivers of Scotland, and carried their knowledge and love of the sport with them to Britain's colonies in the Americas.

Many of these early anglers wrote extensively on their enjoyment of the sport in the colonies, and their accounts fueled interest back home, which led to increasing numbers of anglers after the 1850s. Hunting and fishing were popular diversions and officers traveled extensively throughout Atlantic Canada for their sport.

Two British officers who wrote on their fishing experience in Atlantic Canada were Richard Lewis Dashwood and Campbell Hardy. Dashwood was an officer of the 15th Foot Regiment and left Cork, Ireland, for Saint John, New Brunswick, where he was stationed from 1862 to 1868. He was an avid sportsman who fished and hunted throughout the Maritimes and Newfoundland. Dashwood wrote *Chiploquorgan, or Life by the Campfire in Dominion of Canada and Newfoundland*, which was published in Dublin in 1872. Captain Dashwood was also a keen observer of local fly patterns being used on the rivers of New Brunswick, as evidenced in *Chiploquorgan*:

> The flies for the Nepisiguit are of a plain description, especially as regards the wings, which should be brown mallard, with a few sprigs of golden pheasant neck feather underneath; body fiery brown with blue and claret hackle, wound on together, is a standard fly, and is known by the name of the 'Nicholson,' so called after the inventor, a well-known sportsman of Saint John, New Brunswick. Black body, black hackle and yellow tip is a killer, and the same fly with a crimson tip fishes well at Middle Landing. Grey monkey body and Iris grey hackle is very good in clear water. Body half grey, half claret fur, with grey and claret hackles placed on together, is an admirable fly for the Pabineau (Falls). This fly was invented by my friend Captain Coventry, who stuck many a fish with it off the Flat Rock.

The flies for the Restigouche and its tributaries are rather more gaudy than those used in the Nepisiguit; orange body with claret hackle; body half black, half orange, with black hackle and yellow shoulders; body half black, half crimson, with black hackle and jay shoulder; with all of these mixtures use a rather gaudy mixed wing, with sprigs of wood duck, and red macaw feelers.

The Miramichi, which flows into the Bay of Chaleur, at the town of Chatham, is a fine stream, having many large tributaries, heading far back in the heart of the country. The flies for this river are plain; grey body, with mallard or turkey wings, is one of the standard patterns.

Captain Campbell Hardy was an officer in the Royal Artillery stationed for fifteen years in the Maritimes, much of that time in Halifax. He spent his leaves hunting and fishing, wrote articles for the sporting press, and was the author of two books, *Sporting Adventurers in the New World* (1855) and *Forest Life in Acadie: Sketches of Sport and Natural History in the Lower Provinces of the Canadian Dominion* (1869). In *Sporting Adventures,* Hardy, obviously a great fan of sport fishing, extolled the great sport to be found angling the streams of the eastern British colonies. He wrote that fly fishing was: "all ethereal, vitalizing, elevating. There is nothing gravelly in fly fishing, nothing gross or demoralizing."

Captain Hardy had strong feelings on what was required to be a successful angler on the waters of North America. In *Sporting Adventures*, he expressed his dissatisfaction with the salmon flies available in local stores:

> Every river in Nova Scotia and New Brunswick, has its particular fly, or series of flies adapted for salmon fishing. Some of these flies, particularly those used in the dark streams of Nova Scotia, would be considered monstrous, both as regarded their gaudiness and size, by a sportsman of the old world. Feathers of golden pheasant, Canadian wood-duck, and macaw, show conspicuously amongst the broad plumage of the tail of wild or domestic turkey, on their wings. Their bodies are composed of masses of many-coloured pig's wool, deeply buried in which, are broad bands of tinsel. Others, particularly those for the Atlantic rivers of New Brunswick are smaller, less gaudy, and more carefully made. The dubbing gives place to floss silk, and the turkey wings modestly brightened by a fibre of golden pheasant or scarlet ibis.

Hardy's writing indicates that fly tiers were turning out patterns developed for local rivers but that they were continuing to use traditional fly-tying materials for their salmon flies. It is not surprising that this style of fly tying followed these anglers to the colonies. They were fishing during a period in the second half of the nineteenth century that saw the Atlantic salmon fly become the most complex and challenging aspect of the fly tier's craft. The history of the development of Atlantic salmon flies has been well documented by a variety of angling historians who traced the transition from the first flies, created for pike, grayling and trout, to more complex flies for salmon as fishing tackle improved.

The development of what became known as the gaudy salmon fly is attributed to Irish fly tiers, who were pioneers in the development of bright and complicated

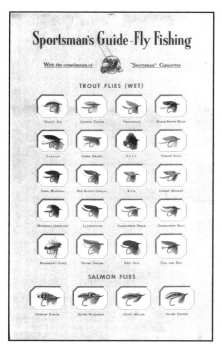

The trout and salmon flies printed on Sportsman Cigarette packages were the only source of fly patterns for many Atlantic Canadian fly tiers.

salmon patterns. These Irish tiers took advantage of silk, silver and gold tinsel, and rare feathers imported for the millinery trade. Despite an initial reluctance on the part of anglers in Scotland and England, by the end of the nineteenth century thousands of fly patterns were in use. Like many aspects of life in Victorian England, flies were required to be complex, overdressed and excessive. The natural history of salmon was not completely understood at this time, so many naturalists believed that salmon continued to feed when they re-entered fresh water. As a result, many early patterns were created to imitate insects such as dragonflies, wasps and butterflies.

Many students of fly-tying history suggest that most salmon flies were intended to imitate butterflies. They point to the fact that the flies had tails, egg sacs (butts), bodies with legs (hackles) heads, feelers (horns) and colourful wings. While there is little evidence in the salmon fishing literature that salmon are attracted to butterflies, there is no question that salmon flies from this period are beautiful and complex. Many present-day anglers continue to fish these traditional featherwing patterns either for their effectiveness or their place in the history of the sport. One of the old favourites which continues to be a popular fly on Atlantic Canadian rivers is the Jock Scott. If tied according to the original dressing, the pattern requires nearly fifty components.

The declaration of the British North America Act on July 1, 1867, which created the Dominion of Canada by joining the former colonies of Upper and Lower Canada, Nova Scotia and New Brunswick, changed the face of angling in Atlantic Canada. Confederation led to the closure of many garrisons and the withdrawal of British troops. While the influence of these early British anglers continued through their writings, their presence on Atlantic Canadian rivers was soon replaced by anglers from the United States. A growing American population was beginning to have an impact on fish and game populations in the eastern states, forcing hunters and anglers to look to Canada for their sport. American anglers soon began moving northward to experience the salmon fishing available in Atlantic Canada.

This began an era that saw grand fishing camps being built in the wilderness, especially in New Brunswick. Like their British counterparts before them, these American anglers were keen to set their exploits in print. One of them, Dean Sage, authored one of the rarest and most sought after books on salmon angling ever printed, *The Restigouche and its Salmon Fishing* (1888).

Sage began fishing the Restigouche around 1875 and his love of the river would eventually lead to the building of a large lodge, Camp Harmony, and the formation

Horse Yachts

A horse yacht was a flat-bottomed scow up to fifty feet long on which a low cabin was built. The cabin was divided into a sleeping area and a kitchen. The yacht was towed up-river by a team of three horses guided by a rider who steered them through water deep enough to float the boat but not too deep for them to wade through. Larger yachts occasionally carried a small jersey cow on the back deck to provide the anglers with fresh milk during the fishing trip. On the horse yachts, anglers traveled up the river for several days, fishing as they went and coming ashore at night to camp. On the trip home the horses would ride on the foredeck.

of the Camp Harmony Angling Club in 1895. Fishing at Camp Harmony was obviously a unique experience that included fine food, drink and comfortable surroundings in a wilderness setting. The luxury did not end at the lodge, either: large scows, known as horse yachts, were used to transport anglers and their equipment up-river and away from the camp for several days of salmon fishing.

These anglers continued to fish with traditional flies and tackle as their British counterparts had done before. While Victorian-style salmon flies continued to be the most popular patterns, featherwing salmon flies were also being developed for Canadian waters. Several of these patterns were designed for fishing the Restigouche River. Two Canadian featherwings, the Night Hawk and Wilmot, were created around 1880 at Camp Harmony, while the Lady Amherst, created around 1925 by George Bonbright, was the most popular pattern on the Restigouche up until 1951 when it lost its title as the big fish fly to two hairwing patterns, the Rusty Rat and Silver Rat.

In the early twentieth century, the fly-tying tide began to turn towards simplicity. One of the leaders of this movement was English author A. H. Chaytor, who discarded any part of the fly he considered unnecessary, such as tails, butts, tags and horns. He even advocated the use of bare hooks under some conditions. This trend is reflected in the Goblin, developed in Newfoundland sometime before 1910 (Bates and Bates Richards). There were several patterns in this series, all having no body material other than the ribbing on a bare black japanned hook.

While the transition from traditional featherwing salmon flies to hairwings didn't happen overnight, change was coming on many rivers of Atlantic Canada, as noted by Jack Anderson of Sherbrooke:

> As a boy growing up on the banks of the St. Mary's River during the late 1920s and 30s, I had a very early introduction to the various types and patterns of salmon flies…the brightly coloured masterpieces of the classic English, Scottish or Irish patterns by such famous makers as S. Alcock, Hardy Brothers, Farlow, etc. One must admit that the beautiful patterns such as the Jock Scott, Lady Amherst, Durham Ranger, Silver Grey, Mar Lodge, and so on are objects of beauty as well as being practical.
>
> These flies were of course very expensive and difficult to obtain, and the local anglers rarely had more than two or three of them at any one time. The eyes of the local fishermen would pop out when we would see the fly books of the more affluent visitors with their expensive collections. Thus, I believe the first locally tied flies were produced for purely financial reasons, rather than desire for new and different patterns…
>
> The materials that went into these flies were very crude—natural deer hair, wool, yarn, cotton thread, shoe maker's wax, tinsel cut from the top of tin tobacco cans, and varnish for head cement. Hook sizes were usually 1, 1/0, 2/0 and 3/0. These same flies were fished throughout the summer without any thought of hook sizes such as # 4, 6 or 8, and they produced results.

There is no question that many of the early patterns came from the hands of Atlantic Canadian tiers. Herbert Howard, a renowned angler, fly tier and angling historian, recalls seeing a family Bible belonging to a Newfoundland family named Stirling, which contained several hand-written entries dated between the years of 1720 and 1896. One of the entries, dated 1795, described a hairwing fly called the Red Cow and says that salmon were caught on it. It is likely that local materials were used to craft flies wherever anglers fly fished for trout and salmon.

Noted author, fly tier and angler Ernest Schwiebert explains the development of simpler salmon flies:

> Canadian fishermen a half century ago were unable to purchase the materials specified in traditional salmon flies, and the cost would have been prohibitive. Similar constraints undoubtedly led simple Scottish flytyers on the remote rivers northeast of Edinburgh, without ready access to major seaports, to develop the more sombre strip-winged Dee patterns and the dark heron-hackled flies popular on the Spey…. 'They're still called guide patterns on some rivers,' commented Colonel Henry Siegel, one of our most knowledgeable angling historians, 'and the guides are proud of the fact that their flies often out-fish the expensive traditionals sold to their sports.'

The growing interest in Atlantic salmon fishing after World War Two led to a rapid increase in the number of fly patterns. The innovation and diversity of Atlantic Canadian fly tiers was recognized by John McDonald in his groundbreaking article in the June 1948 issue of *Fortune* magazine. In the article, "Atlantic Salmon, Accounted the King of Fresh Water Fish," McDonald provides the first exposure to a wider audience for many fly tiers in the region. He obviously went to some lengths to search out fly tiers from throughout eastern North America, with special emphasis on Atlantic Canada, including Ted Bugden and Max Rabbitts from Newfoundland, Joe Aucoin from Nova Scotia and Wallace Doak, Ira Gruber, D. A. LaPointe and Clovis Arsenault from New Brunswick. Both professional and amateur American tiers were also included, such as Lee Wulff, Harry Darbee, Dr. Edwards Park and John Cosseboom.

Dan MacIntosh, shown here with his family and their pet deer, was an early Nova Scotia fly tier. His legacy lives on through his MacIntosh fly.

The fact that salmon flies from Atlantic Canada were beginning to make their mark in the angling world was recognized by Edson Leonard in his landmark book *Flies* (1950), in which he attempted to classify salmon flies:

> One group of flies known as the Margaree type and named after the famous salmon river of the same name is special in that it features hairwings. It follows from this that any standard pattern might be classified as a Margaree if hairwings instead of featherwings are used.

Leonard's efforts to classify hairwing salmon flies as the Margaree type may be due in part to the influence of Cape Breton fly tier Joe Aucoin, who was featured in the book. The "Margaree" name, however, never caught on. Aucoin, like many other tiers of that period, were pioneers in the transition from the old style of tying, characterized by the use of feathers, to the new, which used hair and related elements. This transition was gradual, and is epitomized by one of Aucoin's most popular patterns, the Brown Bomber: Although it has a wing of squirrel tail, it retains many of the characteristics of traditional featherwings such as a peacock herl butt, jungle cock eyes and a veil of golden pheasant.

In part, the transition to locally developed patterns was taking place in the salmon camps and lodges located on Atlantic Canadian rivers. Here, visiting anglers may have arrived with their fly boxes filled with traditional flies, but they soon became convinced of the effectiveness of local patterns. In the guiding busi-

The fly-tying catalogue from the W. W. Doak company in Doaktown, New Brunswick, continues to serve as an important source of salmon fly patterns for many anglers

ness that his family ran on the Gander River in Newfoundland from 1948 until 1965, Brett Saunders came in contact with salmon anglers and flies from around the world, but his choice of flies was rooted in his home waters. In *Rattles and Steadies: Memoirs of a Gander River Man*, written by his son Gary Saunders, Brett relates his experiences guiding salmon anglers:

> They preferred the standard British wet fly tied on a six to number eight hook with a turned up eye. Some fished the tiny number ten, but that was more for the challenge than anything else. The most popular patterns were Dusty Miller, Thunder and Lightning, Black Dose and Blue Charm, all drab looking lures. The most brightly coloured one they used was probably the Silver Doctor, which sported married red, yellow and blue feathers in the wing and fancy silver body winding. Many a novice fisherman protested when his Gander Bay guide took a pocket knife and trimmed such handsome lures down to the essentials—a bit of silver winding on the body, perhaps a wisp of golden pheasant for the tail, some plain brown or speckled black hackle, and a wing stripped of all but the drab colours. But he stopped protesting when he saw the results. The reason the drab colours work better may be that the Gander's pools are shallow. Even the deepest are seldom over six feet in summer. Since salmon rest near the bottom, it could be that, where as in deep they can see bright colours more easily, in the well-lit shallow water the darker colours show up well enough. Whatever the reason, one of the most successful lures of all is the 'moosehair,' a wet fly modeled on the 'black dose,' all black except for its brown wing, yellow tail, and silver winding. About the only time brightly-coloured flies were used was for trouting, usually in May or June month when the sea trout came in. For this such lures as the red and white 'parmachene belle,' the white and brown 'royal coachman' with its peacock body windings, and the red and yellow 'mickey finn' streamer are among the best. But the drab 'black gnat' is good too, especially later in the season.

Few of the early fly tiers in Atlantic Canada had access to books on fly patterns and fly tying. Most of the tiers' knowledge of fly patterns came from seeing actual flies, often given to them as tips by anglers they were guiding. Many a fly tier took the fly apart and made notes and sketches of how they were put together. Many Atlantic Canadian fly tiers consulted Sportsman cigarette packages and the W. W. Doak fishing tackle catalogue for fly patterns.

Joseph D. Bates's *Atlantic Salmon Flies & Fishing* influenced a generation of fly tiers in Atlantic Canada, and another popular title is *Hair Wing Atlantic Salmon Flies*, by Keith Fulsher and Charles Krom.

Other books and publications have followed. *SPAWNER* magazine, the yearly sport fishing magazine produced by the Salmon Preservation Association for the Waters of Newfoundland, made its first appearance in 1979. Twenty-six years later, it continues to profile flies, fly tying and the history of sport fishing, not only in Newfoundland and Labrador but for all of Atlantic Canada. While many anglers in the region subscribed to American hunting and fishing magazines, for many years there were no monthly magazines focusing on this region of Canada. This changed in 1985 with the publication of *Eastern Woods and Waters*, a magazine devoted to hunting and fishing in Atlantic Canada. The magazine recently celebrated its twentieth anniversary and continues to focus on issues important to anglers, hunters and outdoor enthusiasts. Other magazines that have done much to highlight flies and fly tiers in the region are the *Atlantic Salmon Journal* and *Newfoundland Sportsman*, as well as two publications no longer in print, *Maritime Sportsman* and *Cape Breton Outdoors*.

The first book to deal specifically with the flies of Atlantic Canada is Len Rich's *Newfoundland Salmon Flies and How to Tie Them*, which was published in 1985. More recently Dick Stewart's and Farrow Allen's *Atlantic Salmon Flies* (1991) and *Modern Atlantic Salmon Flies* (1998) by Paul Marriner have showcased the innovation and diversity of fly tiers from Atlantic Canada. I realized just how popular hairwing flies from Atlantic Canada had become when I opened a Hardy catalogue in 1984 and found a full page ad devoted to moosehair salmon flies— and not just any salmon flies, but traditional flies such as the Dusty Miller, Jock Scott, Green Highlander and so on.

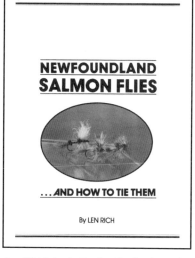

Len Rich's book *Newfoundland Salmon Flies and How to Tie Them* was the first book to profile flies from one region of Atlantic Canada.

There are important differences province to province in fly pattern styles. Traditionally, New Brunswick is known for its black bear patterns tied in the characteristic cigar shape, while Newfoundland tiers prefer smaller flies, mostly tied with moosehair wings. In Nova Scotia, flies tied with native red squirrel wings, as in the style of the MacIntosh series, are common. On Prince Edward Island, shrimp imitations, such as Lester the Lobster, are popular with both trout and salmon anglers.

However, there are also significant differences *within* provinces, between rivers and even sections of rivers. Bill Ensor is well-versed in the diversity of fly-tying styles in New Brunswick. As the retired manager of promotion for fishing and hunting in New Brunswick, Ensor has fished and guided for trout and salmon throughout the province. Between the Restigouche and the Miramichi, NB's two largest river system, Ensor notes a difference in the flies: "Flies on the Restigouche tend to be green, the Green Highlander and Cosseboom being two popular patterns. On the other hand, fish on the Miramichi prefer darker flies." Size also varies: "Anglers usually fish flies which are a size or two larger on the Restigouche than on the Miramichi."

In Nova Scotia, May Fly Tackle Shop associate Fred Harrigan also noticed a difference according to region and sometimes river to river: "The Cosseboom was popular in Cape Breton and the eastern part of the province, but it was mostly silver flies they liked on the South Shore rivers. It could change within twenty miles. What they used in one river they wouldn't have any luck with in the next."

EASTERN WOODS & WATERS, SPRING, 1985 $2.50
Giant Labrador trout
Are cormorants hurting game fish?
Crows for off-season shooting
Floating those dry flies
Lee Wulff on releasing salmon
Fishing with nymphs: it's easy

Atlantic Canada's own outdoor magazine

The publication of *Eastern Woods and Waters* magazine in 1985 provided a forum to showcase the flies and fly tiers of Atlantic Canada.

Newfoundland is no different, according to Don Hutchens: "Streamers are popular on the west coast rivers, while anglers in Central Newfoundland and the Avalon Peninsula tend to prefer more traditional patterns such as the Blue Charm, Thunder and Lightning and so on."

Today, on Atlantic Canadian lakes and rivers, old favourites such as the Thunder and Lightning, Blue Charm, Cosseboom or Black Bear series are still popular, while new patterns with names like Slime, Canary and Popsicle are showing up on many rivers. These flies are about as far removed as possible from the traditional patterns. Regional differences are becoming less pronounced as technology changes how information is transferred. With the popularity of internet fly-tying sites and bulletin boards, a hot pattern on the Miramichi today may show up on the Gander or Margaree tomorrow.

While we celebrate the history of flies and fly fishing for trout and salmon, we recognize that sport fishing is changing and fly tiers are changing with it. Trout and salmon will probably always be the species of choice but new species, new fly-tying materials, and new tiers combine to create a growing and vibrant community of fly tiers. The diversity and innovation that mark fly tying in Atlantic Canada lives on.

Chapter 2

Fly Tiers of New Brunswick

"New Brunswick is, in my opinion, the headquarters for the fly fisherman. This province is intersected in every direction by large rivers. It abounds in fine clear and rapid streams, of easy access, and on which the scenery is of the most magnificent description in North America.

Campbell Hardy
Sporting Adventures in the New World *(1855)*

Restigouche, Miramichi, Upsalquitch, Dungarvon, Sevogle, Renous and Nepisiguit—for Atlantic salmon anglers, mere mention of these rivers brings to mind dark forests, bright water and silver salmon. With three great rivers—the St. John, Miramichi and Restigouche—supporting strong runs of Atlantic salmon, New Brunswick has a long history of fly fishing and tying. In villages along the banks of these rivers and their tributaries, New Brunswick fly tiers such as Clovis Arsenault, Wally Doak, Abe Munn, and many others quietly tied flies designed to match conditions on local rivers. Their flies, crafted with materials from farmyard and forest, laid the framework for a new age of salmon flies.

The Miramichi and Restigouche are still renowned for their salmon runs, with the Miramichi supporting the largest number of returning salmon of any river in North America. The St. John, unfortunately, is a shadow of its former self due to problems ranging from hydro development to poor at-sea survival.

Atlantic salmon are the most popular sport fish in New Brunswick, but brook trout are a close second, and most of the lakes in the province's interior support great fishing. Many of the salmon rivers also have good runs of sea-run brook trout, which enter the rivers with the first rise of water in late spring and early summer. Today the St. John is a world-class destination for angling small-mouth bass and muskellunge. American shad and striped bass are also popular with fly-fishing anglers, and brown trout are found in a few areas of the province.

Joseph Clovis Arsenault

1902–1980

Best known as the creator of the Rusty Rat fly, J. Clovis Arsenault was one of the pioneering fly tiers in Atlantic Canada. Born in Black Cape, Quebec, he moved to Atholville, New Brunswick, in 1929. His fly tying, which began as a hobby, turned into a business in the 1930s when he began tying flies for members of the Restigouche Salmon Club.

The Rusty Rat fly has been credited to several sources, but Joseph Bates and Pamela Bates Richards prove that it resulted from the collaborative efforts of Clovis Arsenault and Joseph Pulitzer. In a 1965 issue of the *Atlantic Salmon Journal*, entitled "A Salute to the Three Rats," Sam Day quotes Clovis in reference to the creation of the Rusty Rat:

> It was in 1949, and the late Joseph Pulitzer had been fishing with one of my large Black Rats. It happened that I had used a rusty floss for the under binding and after he'd taken a salmon or two the fly was pretty well chewed up, the body torn and the rusty tying thread had been cut and came through. But, as is often the case the more disreputable the fly became in appearance the more alluring it must have been to the salmon for Mr. Pulitzer wound up with a 41 pounder.
>
> He came back to me excited about its performance and enthusiastic about its possibilities. He handed me what remained of the fly and told me he wanted it copied exactly. I got to work and after several tries produced a fly that pleased him, and immediately named it the Rusty Rat.

Clovis's flies were featured in publications ranging from *Life* magazine in 1942 to John McDonald's salmon article in the June 1948 issue of *Fortune* magazine. McDonald included two flies tied by Arsenault, a Silver Gray and the Black Jack. From all accounts Arsenault was an innovative fly tier, using various materials ranging from moose to monkey hair to make his flies.

Bob Baker

Bob was born in Middleton, Nova Scotia, in 1938. Although he did some fishing when he was growing up, his local river, the Nictaux, was dammed for hydro development at that time, and its once great salmon run stopped. Bob's fly tying and fishing began at an early age: "I can remember when I was around twelve, I tied a fly using a bait hook, thread and some hair from our dog. I went to the river with the fly and hooked a trout that wrapped itself around a stick and eventually got off. I can remember being upset that my father didn't go out and get the fish off the stick. There was only about ten feet of water in that spot."

Bob's salmon fishing began in earnest when he moved to

New Brunswick and hooked his first fish on the Nepisiguit River, which he lost. And while the first fish he landed was on the Jacquet, it was on the Nepisiguit that Bob would develop his love for fishing, fly tying and salmon. Bob credits his neighbour in Bathurst, George Casey, with teaching him fly tying. He also found books like *Master Fly Tying Guide* by Art Flick to be useful.

Conversation with Bob always turns back to his beloved Nepisiguit River. "There are only about eighteen miles that are fishable," he says, "and in 1880 the fishing on that section leased for $200 a year. In comparison the South-West Miramichi leased for only $50. The fishing was that good." A chemical spill in 1969 devastated the river and its trout and salmon; however, through hard work on the part of local sport fishing groups, the river has been restored to its former greatness and now supports a quality fishery.

Bob is an innovative fly tier who enjoys experimenting with materials and developing new patterns. He gets his inspiration from many sources. One of his fly patterns, the Shadow series, was inspired by a poem by New Brunswick poet Chris Grant, in particular the line, "shadows hang suspended in the water's changing light." Bob first fished the fly on the Jacquet River when the water temperature was four degrees Celsius and hooked fourteen fish that day. In recognition of the twenty-five-pound salmon on one of his flies during a solar eclipse, he christened the fly the Eclipse. Bob has developed about twenty named fly series over the years and fishes them all. "Not all of the patterns I have come up with are successful," says Bob, "and unless they catch fish I don't name them."

Bob ties on a variety of hooks including Mustad and Partridge. For display flies, he says, you can't beat the Bartleet. A strong believer in fishing with barbless hooks, he has been tying his flies this way for years, tying to match water conditions, using heavier dressings for high water and switching to sparser flies for low water conditions. But he insists there are no hard-and-fast rules for fly tying. "I caught salmon on a #10 fly in high water and on a #2 in low water. You have to be adaptable to match what the fish want that day." Bob has written on fly tying and fly fishing for a variety of publications such as *SPAWNER* magazine and the *Atlantic Salmon Journal*. He contributed a section on New Brunswick rivers to *A Master's Guide to Atlantic Salmon Fishing* by Bill Cummings, and his flies appeared in Paul Marriner's book, *Modern Atlantic Salmon Flies*.

Shadow

Thread:	White	Rib:	Oval gold tinsel over black only
Tag:	Oval gold, three turns		
Tip:	Fluorescent orange	Wing:	Black squirrel over several strands green Krystal Flash
Tail:	Claret over golden pheasant crest		
Butt:	Black ostrich	Hackle:	Black, three turns
Body:	Black phentex three quarters, with remaining orange Krystal Flash	Head:	Black

Danny Bird

Danny was born in Fredericton, New Brunswick, in 1950. He began fly tying when he was a teenager. "A neighbour, Ernie Hall, taught me the basics and I have been tying ever since," he says. Danny is well known among fly tiers in Atlantic Canada for a number of his patterns, including the Glitter Bug, which he came up with in 1978 after attending a fly-fishing show in Pennsylvania. It was the first time he saw Krystal Flash. He took some home and used it to tie the Glitter Bug, which he fished for a couple of years with some success before other anglers found out what he was using.

Danny is a fan of traditionally shaped flies: "I want a fly to have a nice tapered head and be tied in the traditional style with a fairly full body. Most of the hair wings can be traced back to traditional feather wings so there is not really that much new in fly tying." He ties his salmon flies on a Tiemco hook, #7099, which has a black Japan finish: "It's a lovely hook; it makes the fly, in my opinion."

An avid angler and fly tier, in his spare time Danny's working life also revolves around Atlantic salmon. As the regional director for the Atlantic Salmon Federation, Danny is involved on a daily basis with issues relating to sport-fish conservation and management.

Michael Brislain

Michael was born in Montreal in 1947 and grew up in the Eastern Townships. He later moved to Nova Scotia and finally Fredericton, where he now lives. Although Michael began fishing when he was four years old in the lakes and streams of Quebec, his first experience fly fishing came in 1971 in Nova Scotia. A co-worker took him salmon fishing on the Stewiacke River and, as Michael describes it, he was hooked.

He began fly tying shortly after, picking it up on his own and with the help of Ernest Schwiebert's book *Nymphs*. Another book that Michael found helpful was Alf Walker's *Mastering the Art and Craft of Tying Atlantic Salmon Flies*. Michael is perhaps best known for his own book, *Bugging the Atlantic Salmon*.

Meg's Special

Tag:	Oval gold tinsel		Rib:	Oval gold tinsel
Butt:	Orange floss or wool		Wing:	Five to six strands of orange Krystal Flash with an overwing of black squirrel tail
Tail:	Golden pheasant crest followed by second butt of black ostrich herl			
Body:	Several strands of orange Krystal Flash		Hackle:	Orange, tied collar-style

Green Envy/L'Envie Verte

Hook:	Partridge 2, 4, 6,	Cheeks:	Jungle Cock (optional)
Tag:	Fine Oval Gold Tinsel	Wing:	2/3 white calf tail with
Tail:	Golden Pheasant Rump		1/3 green squirrel tail
	Feather		over and golden pheas-
Ribbing:	Medium Oval Gold Tinsel		ant rump feather notched
Under			over green squirrel tail
Body:	Floss overlaid with pea-	Hackle:	Highlander Green Fly Pat-
	cock herl		tern

Michael's interest in the bug and bomber started in 1982, when he was fishing the St. John River. "There was one angler there who was catching fish when no one else was. He was fishing a brown bug, a #6, with a red butt, natural deer hair spun on and trimmed for the body and a brown hackle palmered through it." Michael's interest in the pattern resulted in further study of the fly and its effectiveness: "Its neutral buoyancy is the key to its effectiveness. It floats right in the surface film," he says.

Michael gets great satisfaction from fly tying and has caught all of his salmon on flies he tied himself. He is a careful tier who likes to take his time, using the best hooks and materials to make the best fly he can.

Proportions are important. He likes a fly to be well-proportioned and not too heavily dressed. In his opinion, a sparse fly fishes better than a heavily dressed one. Originally Michael tied his bombers on Partridge DS4 hooks but now uses Partridge's CS42. He uses a variety of materials for tying his Bugs and Bombers, including white-tail deer, moose and caribou hair for bodies. In addition to a tail of calftail, he often adds a split wing calftail wing, especially on bombers for the rivers of the Gaspé.

Michael laments the decline of his home river, the St. John, which he fished for twenty years. "When I began fishing here there was a run of thirty thousand fish and it was nothing to see a hundred boats on the river. Last year the return to the Mactaquac Dam was about six hundred fish." These days Michael fishes the Miramichi and the York River on the Gaspé Peninsula in Quebec. The green waters

"In New Brunswick, according to many guides and outfitters, there is a decided preference for single-hook flies, in sizes from No.2 to No.10. Some anglers have individual preferences for non-standard patterns but usually the old stand-bys get good results. These include the Silver Doctor, Parmachene Belle, Jock Scott, Montreal, Brown and Gray hackle, and the Black Gnat. The Wulff dry flies, and the Brown Bivisible, Pink Lady, all on sizes 8, 10 and 12 hooks, are also popular. When the water is low, the standard low-water salmon flies are used: sparsely tied, small flies, on size 10 and 12 hooks. Best patterns are the Silver Doctor, Black Doctor, Black Dose, Silver Gray, Thunder and Lightening, Jock Scott, and Blue Charm."

Joe Brooks, *Complete Guide to Fishing Across North America* (1966)

of the York were the inspiration for the fly he contributed for this book, a pattern of his own design he calls the Green Envy/L'Envie Verte.

Renate Bullock

Renate was born in Germany in 1945 and immigrated to Saint John, New Brunswick, with her parents in 1953. Her introduction to fly fishing came in 1966 when she and her husband spent their honeymoon at a salmon camp in Boisetown. They returned to the camp every year to celebrate their anniversary and eventually bought the camp in 1973. At first they used it as a summer home and spent the season there, but in 1985 they moved there permanently.

To Renate, fly fishing is magical. Her love of, and interest in, fly fishing for salmon led her to fly tying in the 1980s. Her main impetus came from a desire to have the flies she wanted, when she needed them. "If the river came up or dropped, I wanted to have the flies I needed to match water conditions and I didn't want to have to wait to get them from someone else," laughs Renate. At that time Renate and her husband leased the salmon pools at their camp to outfitter Vince Swazey. "Vince, as well as his clients, were a big help to me when I began fly tying," recalls Renate. She credits well-known Saint John tier Warren Duncan with teaching her much of what she knows about tying salmon flies. She was also fortunate to tie with Bob Warren of Massachusetts. "Bob was a guest at Vince's camp and he was very willing to share his knowledge with me."

Renate acknowledges the benefits she received from several books on tying Atlantic salmon flies, citing *Fishing Atlantic Salmon* and Dick Stewart's and Farrow Allen's *Flies for Atlantic Salmon*.

Her approach to flying is simple: "If you are catching fish then you know that you have tied the right fly." She likes her flies to be sparse, not over dressed, but she believes the proportions are important.

The RBM

Hook:	Mustad 3665A or 9575	Wing:	Four strands fine, flat pearl flashabou, then four strands oval pearl Krystal Flash
Tag:	#14 UNI-Mylar flat silver tinsel		
Body:	Underwrap with silver Mylar. Green (light or mid green) Gordon Griffiths floss or comparable. Variations such as back half tied green, front half orange will work, but not as well as the original	Collar:	Black hen feather under unclipped tips of black deer hair pointing to the point
		Head:	Black dyed deer body hair, spun, packed and clipped, trimmed to a small conical muddler shape
Rib:	#14 UNI-Mylar tinsel from the tag		

Among her favourites are her own RBM, the Butterfly, a very popular fly on the Miramichi, and finally The Same Thing Murray, tied with a light green body instead of the usual yellow. The RBM is special because it is tied with a Muddler head, which she finds effective. "On the RBM I added a collar of hackle since I find that deer hair, when it is dyed black, tends to be more brittle than the natural hair. So, when the deer hair collar eventually breaks off, I still have a collar formed by the hackle."

Renate ties on a Regal vice and favours Tiemco hooks for her salmon flies: "They are very sharp, and I find that they remain sharp while you are fishing so you don't have to touch them up as often." She ties flies commercially for her clients and purchases most of her supplies from Warren Duncan. Her long-time clients also keep her supplied with materials. One of her favourite materials is Gordon Griffith floss: "It lies flat and doesn't fray," claims Renate, "and it comes in a wide variety of colours."

Renate's love of fishing led her to become a fishing guide in 1977. "We had family who visited us from Germany and they often wanted to go fishing for a day or two while they were staying with us so I thought that I would get my guiding licence so I could take them out," she recalls. Eventually her neighbour, Vince Swazey, asked her to guide for his outfitting business and she has been guiding ever since. Renate spends most of the salmon season on the water, and that time has provided her with a lot of experience and insight on what attracts a salmon to the fly. She keeps a daily log in which she records information on air and water temperature, whether the day was bright or dark, clear or raining, what flies were used, and which were successful.

"Both the fly and the presentation are important," she says. "You need a fly sized to match water conditions but you must also present it to the fish properly. That is where I see experienced salmon anglers have an advantage. There are subtle differences in how they fish compared to a new angler. They expect to catch fish and are prepared when a fish takes so they know what to do." Renate stresses that "the only way to get experience is to fish and there is no substitute for spending time out on the water, fishing."

Renate is pleased that one of her sons, Dan Bullock, has taken over the outfitting business and will run it as Tuckaway Cabins. She will continue to guide, tie flies, and enjoy the magic.

Catherine Lynn Colford

Cathy was born in the Lac Saint-Jean area of Quebec in 1958. Both her parents were from the Blackville area of New Brunswick, so she grew up hearing about the Miramichi and spent summers there. She moved back to New Brunswick in 1976. Her fly tying began around 2001, when she began working for Brock Curtis at his store, Miramichi River Outfitters: "The flies really captivated me, all the different sizes, colours and patterns. I was especially taken with the flies which Marc

Handsome Dude

Butt:	Chartreuse	Rib:	Small oval gold
Tail:	Grey squirrel	Hackle:	Brown
Body:	Peacock herl	Wing:	Grey squirrel, tied low

Madore tied for the shop. Marc's flies were art on a hook as far as I was concerned. Brock and Marc decided that I should start tying flies and I was anxious to learn. Marc began to teach me the basics of fly tying, and my first fly was a Green Machine, a standard on local waters. From there I went on to tie Bombers, Butterflies and Whiskers."

The Handsome Dude is one of her favourites. It is a variation of the whiskers to which she adds a gold rib and a chartreuse butt. She says that colour seems to add something extra to a fly.

Cathy continues to take fly-tying lessons from Marc Madore. "Marc is my mentor as well as a friend. He has great patience and makes each lesson interesting and fun." Cathy has tied at the Fly Fishing Forum in Granby, Quebec where she was the only woman among the sixteen fly tiers entered. She also attended the Dieppe Fly Fishing show in New Brunswick.

As a commercial tier, Cathy has favourite materials. One of them is calf body hair. "I find the calf body hair is straighter than hair from the tail. I use it mainly for wings on my butterflies and find it lays nice and straight."

While she continues her commercial tying, Cathy will soon add guiding to her duties.

Rev. L. E. Davis

1913–1966

L. E. Davis was born in Dauphin, Manitoba, but moved to Shelburne, Nova Scotia, with his family when he was a boy. He graduated from Acadia University in 1935 and became a Baptist minister. He served in several churches in Nova Scotia before moving to St. Stephen, New Brunswick, in 1949. His son, Jack Davis, believes that his father began tying flies in the 1940s but not seriously until after his move to St. Stephen.

Rev. Davis was known for several original fly patterns, among them the Bone Crusher and the St. Croix series. Jack remembers

Bone Crusher

Tail:	Lady Amherst Pheasant Tippet (two black bars showing)	Wing:	White Marabou extending just beyond the bend of the hook.
Body:	Red Wool	Head:	Black
Throat:	Orange Calf Tail		

his father tying the St. Croix Yellow, St. Croix Pride, St. Croix Grey and St. Croix Red, although he was never a high-volume fly tier: "He sold enough to buy his Orvis rods and other fishing equipment," says Jack. Rev. Davis sold his flies in local shops as well as in Maine. Also an avid angler, he fished for trout, landlocked salmon, Atlantic salmon and striped bass.

He tied trolling streamers for landlocked salmon—all the popular Maine patterns: Wardens Worry, Green King and Nine-Three. He also fly fished for striped bass in the St. Croix River, and had considerable success on stripers trolling streamers behind his boat.

According to Jack, Rev. Davis purchased supplies mostly from Herers, and ordered hooks from Hardy in England. "He used to test the point of the hook by flicking it with his thumbnail. If it pinged the right way, he was satisfied that it was tempered properly and would be strong enough to hold a fish so he would tie a fly with it. If it didn't sound right it was discarded."

The Bone Crusher fly marks an important innovation in fly tying as it was one of the first to use marabou as wing material. Today, marabou flies are very popular, especially for fall salmon fishing, and most salmon anglers have a selection of marabou flies, with names like Popsicle, Grape or the Canary in their fly box.

W. W. (Wallace) Doak

1913–1979

For those of us who tie a few dozen flies each year for our own use or for friends, it is hard to imagine producing five thousand flies a year, and even harder to imagine maintaining that production level for fifty years. In his fifty-year career as a commercial fly tier, Wallace Doak from Doaktown, New Brunswick, played an important role in popularizing the flies and fly tying styles of Atlantic Canada.

The Atlantic Salmon Museum in Doaktown, which honours Wallace Doak in a display featuring his life and flies, tells us that he developed his fly-tying skills by observing another local tier, D'Arcy O'Donnell, a Doaktown barber. While he developed his own retail business, Wallace wholesaled flies to established stores, including James S. Neil's in Fredericton and McCloskey's in Boston. During this period of his life he was also employed as a mill worker, lumberman and fishing guide. Gradually, however, his business grew and increasing demand for his flies forced him to begin tying full-time.

Wallace Doak and his flies have been featured in many magazine articles and books. His son, Jerry, who continues the tradition of tying good flies begun by his father, told me that his father was a quiet man. "He approached fly tying in a practical manner and resisted the temptation to develop new flies. He felt there were already enough flies and instead he concentrated on producing neat and durable versions of established patterns. He built his reputation through the quality and consistency of his product. It is a reputation we work hard to maintain to this day."

Jerry Doak

Jerry was born in Doaktown in 1956. As the son of legendary New Brunswick fly tier Wallace Doak, he grew up in the family business. When his father passed away in 1979, Jerry took over the fly-tying shop. Today the shop employs two additional full-time tiers, Bruce Waugh and John Lyons, and does a busy retail and mail order business. Many fly tiers throughout Atlantic Canada cite the W. W. Doak fly shop as the source for much of their fly-tying material.

Jerry continues the tradition of tying fine fishing flies begun by his father. His work has been featured in numerous books and magazine articles, and a Lady Amherst fly tied by Jerry was featured by Canada Post in their 1998 collection of fishing flies.

Jerry Doak's Lady Amherst salmon fly.

To Jerry, durability and consistency are critical elements of his fly tying: "Every tier has a vision in their mind of what makes a good fly. How consistently you can match that vision is a mark of a good tier. If the hundredth fly you tie looks identical to the first one, then you are turning out consistent flies."

While the Undertaker and the Green Machine are two of the store's most popular flies, Jerry's personal favourite is the Oriole, developed by Ira Gruber: "It is a featherwing, which is practical but not flamboyant. It incorporates the fly-tying styles of early tiers such as Charlie DeFeo and Ira Gruber and to my way of thinking is an evocative fly from a bygone era."

Warren Duncan

Warren, or "Dunc" as he is affectionately known, was born in Campbellton, New Brunswick, in 1948. Warren fished as a young boy, but his fly fishing began when he moved to Saint John and learned that there were salmon in the local Hammond River. "If you wanted to fish for salmon you had to fly fish, so I began fly fishing in 1971," says Dunc.

His fly tying began around the same time: "I bought a fly tying kit at Woolco, a Worth Fly Tying Kit, which sold for $4.95. I began tying flies and kept at it for several years when I saw an advertisement for Bill Hunter's store in New Boston, New Hampshire. I went down and we became friends. Bill taught me a lot of the tricks of the trade, which improved my fly tying. I also met some great fly tiers through Bill, including Dave Whitlock and Poul Jorgensen."

While Dunc cites a number of important books in helping with his fly tying, including Art Flick's *Master Fly Tying Guide* and especially *Atlantic Salmon Flies and Fishing*, he also credits his friendship with Paul Schmookler. "Paul taught me a lot about selecting and grading quality fly-tying materials in order to have the best for tying flies."

Dunc operated a retail fly shop out of his house in the 1970s; in 1985, he moved to his present location. Dunc first began tying flies commercially for Hunter's shop as well as L. L. Bean and Orvis. He also ties for Ramsey Outdoor Stores in New Jersey. Dunc is so busy filling his commercial and custom orders that he has no flies available for sale in his shop. "I hope to change that, now that I am retired," he laughs. Dunc also travelled down to the United States to conduct fly-tying workshops at Bill Hunter's store, and since then has conducted workshops on tying hair-wing Atlantic salmon as far away as California, as well as Scotland, Denmark, England and Norway. In addition he hosted a television series on fly tying which was broadcast on Maine Public Television. He is well known throughout Canada for his fly-tying classes.

In 1992, I attended Dunc's workshop at the Atlantic Salmon Conclave held on the St. Mary's River in Nova Scotia. His skill and humour left a big impression and encouraged me to improve my own fly tying. I learned that Dunc has cut a wide swath across the fly-tying circuit in Atlantic Canada. Many fly tiers interviewed for this book told me that Dunc, either through his workshops or his television show, had been a big help to them with their fly tying.

Depending on water conditions, temperature, and time of day, Dunc uses a variety of flies for his own fishing. He fishes the Miramichi as well as the Restigouche and is a member of a fly-fishing club that leases fishing on a trout lake near Saint John. "I am a much better fly tier than I am a fisherman," he laughs, "but I get a great deal of enjoyment from it." Dunc is an active supporter of angling groups, including the local Hammond River Angling Association. The runs on the local St. John River have declined in recent years, but Dunc says there are other angling opportunities available, from brown trout and striped bass to muskies and small-mouth bass.

Dunc's flies have been featured in a wide variety of books and magazines ranging from *Fly Tyer* magazine to the *Atlantic Salmon Journal*. The *Art of Angling Journal* featured a stunning display of his flies. His flies have appeared in several noteworthy books, including *Rare and Unusual Fly Tying Materials* by Paul Schmookler and Ingrid Sils, and *Fishing Atlantic Salmon* by Joseph Bates and Pamela Bates-Richards.

Dunc is well known for several fly patterns which have proved their worth on Atlantic salmon rivers around the world. He is probably best known for the Undertaker, but is quick to say that the fly came from several sources: "I took the

Dunc's Smelt

Body:	Underwrap of pearl Mylar tinsel, then covered with pearl Mylar tubing, frayed at end to form a tail	Wing:	Peacock herl over gray bucktail over white bucktail
Cheeks:	Jungle cock (optional)	Throat:	Grizzly hackle

name from a fly which Quebec fly tier Joe Dugay used to tie in the 1940s. Joe died and the pattern was lost, but I liked the name so when Chris Russell gave me a fly to copy, I used peacock herl for the body and named it the Undertaker."

He has also created Dunc's Shrimp, Dunc's Smelt and a bomber pattern he calls the Coyote. When asked how to tie the latter, Dunc replies, "It is all deer hair, from the tail and wing to the body, which is palmered with a brown hackle."

Another of Dunc's flies is a tribute to his home province: "Bill Ensor, who worked for the New Brunswick Tourism Department, asked me to come up with a fly that would symbolize New Brunswick. The only directions he gave me were that the fly had to include two colours, fiddlehead green and cranberry red. The result was a fly I called The Picture Province."

Bryant Freeman

Well known as the owner and operator of Escape Anglers in Riverview, New Brunswick, Bryant casts a long shadow in the world of Atlantic Canadian fly tying. He was born along the banks of Nova Scotia's Medway River in the community of Greenfield in 1941. As the son of Lew Freeman, a well-known angler and fly tier himself (see Chapter 4), it wasn't long before Bryant was fishing the Medway and tying flies: "I used to help Dad tie flies when I was just a kid," Bryant told me. "He lost his arm in a sawmill accident when he was a young man and I used to hold the wings on the hook as he tied it on."

Bryant remembers catching his first salmon from the Medway River when he was only ten years old. "I caught it on a Silver Gray," he recalls. "In those days the first bright salmon would appear in the Medway in early April. The Silver Gray was the most popular fly on the river and you could leave it on until May 15 when everyone switched to fishing dry flies. We really only needed one [dry] fly. It was a variation of the MacIntosh pattern and consisted of a golden pheasant tippett, peacock herl body, red squirrel tail wing and brown hackle."

Bryant's early experiences were with Hardy flies and tackle—the Hardy Rogue River was the most popular rod at the time, and they fished with King Eider silk HCH, double taper lines. As a result of his skill as an angler, Bryant was guiding salmon anglers by the time he was fourteen years old, mostly for the Freeman House, a hotel that catered to anglers fishing the Medway.

Bryant graduated from vocational school in 1960 and joined Canadian National Railways in Northern New Brunswick where he worked as a telecommunications technician until he retired in 1991. Living in New Brunswick allowed him to continue his interest in salmon fishing and fly tying. It was during this time that he developed the Rabbi fly: "I caught my first Miramichi salmon on that pattern and it has been a favourite ever since. I kept that particular fly and fished it for fifteen years. The hook was getting thin at the end," he laughs.

Bryant's work allowed him to travel throughout the province and he was seldom without his fishing gear. In 1967, he became interested in tying featherwing Atlan-

The Atlantic Salmon Museum in Doaktown, New Brunswick, highlights the important role salmon continues to play in the life of New Brunswick.

The Atlantic Salmon Museum

The Atlantic Salmon Museum, formerly known as the Miramichi Salmon Museum, is located on the banks of the Main South West Miramichi River in the village of Doaktown. Through a series of displays, art work, live interpreters, and a video presentation, the museum tells the story of Atlantic salmon in New Brunswick, and the anglers, guides, outfitters and fly tiers who have forged an important part of its history in the province.

On display at the museum are the works of many well-known fly tiers, as well as fishing gear ranging from rods and reels to canoes and gaffs. The art gallery on the lower level is also well stocked with angling art by current and past masters. While its main emphasis is on angling, the museum also highlights the environment of the Miramichi River watershed. An aquarium displays a variety of local fish species and other aquatic life as well as Atlantic salmon through the various stages of their life cycle.

The museum plays an active role in the community through programs like "Come Play In the River," which introduces young people to angling and the natural history of the Miramichi River.

The Rabbi

Tail:	Golden pheasant tippets	Wing:	Red squirrel
Butt:	Black ostrich herl	Hackle:	Brown, collared
Body:	Green wool or seal fur	Head:	Red
Rib:	Silver tinsel		

tic salmon flies, which he refers to as traditionals (as opposed to classics). He finds John Veniard's fly-tying guide, *The Fly Dressers Guide*, very useful.

Bryant's interest in fly tying soon led him into the commercial side of the business when he began tying flies for several New Brunswick shops, mostly hairwings for Frank Rickard and fully dressed traditional salmon flies for Wally Doak.

Bryant opened Escape Anglers in 1985, and it continues to be a must-stop for salmon anglers on their way to fish the Miramichi or the Gaspé rivers. His work to conserve Atlantic salmon has been recognized by a variety of organizations. In 1997, the New Brunswick Salmon Council and the Atlantic Salmon Federation honoured Bryant for his contributions to the sport of angling for Atlantic salmon in New Brunswick by distinguishing himself in the art of crafting and designing Atlantic salmon flies. He has served on the New Brunswick Salmon Council, Nelson Hollow Salmon Association, Petitcodiac River Keepers and as editor of the Barbless Butterfly, the New Brunswick Salmon Council's newsletter. But perhaps the highest praise comes from his fellow fly tiers and anglers. Dewey Gillespie, author of *Where the Rivers Meet: The Fly Tyers of New Brunswick* and creator of a website devoted to fly tiers from that province, he had glowing praise for Bryant and his contribution to fly tying: "Ted Williams had a saying about people who impressed him, he called them 'A Big League Guy' and in my books Bryant Freeman is a 'Big League Guy.'"

Dewey Gillespie

Dewey was born in Blackville, New Brunswick, in 1952. He joined the Blackville Police Department in 1976 and later moved to the

"Anglers who fish anywhere on the vast network of the Miramichi usually drive north through Doaktown, which is famous mainly because Wally Doak lives there. Wally is proprietor of a neat little tackle shop on the main street, and it is customary to drop in to learn about new styles in flies; to purchase tackle; to inquire how the river is; and to find out who's around and what is going on."

Joseph D. Bates Jr.,
Atlantic Salmon Flies and Fishing (1970)

force in Newcastle, now the Miramichi Police Force, where he serves as an investigator. Growing up on the banks of the Miramichi River near Doctors Island Pool, Dewey began salmon fishing at an early age and caught his first salmon when he was eleven years old. His father was a well-known outfitter and Dewey remembers many well-known anglers such as Charles DeFeo and Ted Williams visiting the family home. Dewey began fly tying around the time he caught his first salmon and remembers receiving a fly-tying badge in Scouts when he was twelve. Years later, he would present that same badge to his twelve-year-old son. While Dewey never tied commercially, anglers and fly tiers owe him a great debt of gratitude because of his work as a historian and writer. His book, *Where the Rivers Meet: The Fly Tyers of New Brunswick*, is the first to focus on the fly tiers of Atlantic Canada.

The book began with a trip to the salmon museum in Doaktown, where Dewey was impressed with the displays on the old-time fly tiers such as Wallace Doak and Bert Miner and with the framed flies. Dewey began his research by reading all the books on salmon fishing that he could find and noting which New Brunswick fly tiers and flies were mentioned. He began cataloguing the various tiers and framing their flies. His neighbour, Jean Patineau, was an artist and also had a framing business. Another friend, John Henderson, a master fly tier, provided the flies. Eventually he had enough material to put on a show; the first one took place in Moncton in 1993. The show toured throughout the province until 1998.

Dewey's book was a product of his research for the show and is now, unfortunately, out of print; nevertheless, Dewey continues his research, which he makes available on the internet. The site will eventually have one hundred fly tiers. Crediting fly fishing and fly tying for many good things in his life, including receiving the Queens Jubilee Medal, he is quick to acknowledge the people who have helped him in his efforts to preserve the fly tying history of New Brunswick, notably Bud L. Kitchen and Bryant Freeman.

Ira Gruber

1889–1962

Ira Gruber was a pioneer in the development of hairwing flies for Atlantic salmon in Atlantic Canada. An American, he owned a

"What does a salmon prefer? After fifty years I have decided that it is the fly you fish with, be it whatever pattern you use. The thing is to keep your fly in the water. In other words, fish. On one occasion I used the same fly for three consecutive days, only taking it off to retie the leader when it became frayed. The fly was a Mar Lodge; but I am convinced that almost any other—of the right size—would have done as well. I hooked and landed five fish—all big."
George Frederick Clarke, Six Salmon Rivers and Another (1960)

knitting mill in Spring Valley, Pennsylvania, until he retired to New Brunswick in 1915 to spend the rest of his life hunting and fishing. From all accounts Ira was an avid angler, fishing almost every day during the season and often using two rods. If he hooked a fish he would pass the rod to his guide and go back to fishing with the second rod while his guide played the fish.

Ira began tying flies in 1935 under the guidance of local tier Everitt Price. Together they created over twenty patterns that contributed to the conversion of salmon flies from traditional featherwings to hairwing flies.

"Ira, more than anyone else, was responsible for developing the general configuration of the Miramichi-style salmon fly with its short, cigar shaped body, ribbed with fine, close-turned tinsel and with a wing which was short and hugged the body. Another feature of his style was the care with which throat hackle was tied in or wound on" (Bates).

Ira was also a pioneer in fishing small flies for salmon in low water. Prior to his experiences with small flies, most anglers stopped fishing in low water because the fish were too difficult to catch. He was able to show that he could catch salmon at this time of year by using flies tied on small hooks, down to #12. Only a few of Ira's patterns continue to be fished on the Miramichi these days. One of his most popular flies, which continues to be included in the W. W. Doak catalogue, is the Oriole, a featherwing pattern.

Doug Haney

Doug was born in 1950 in St. Stephen, New Brunswick, and has lived there all his life. He fished for trout as a boy and began fishing for salmon when he was around sixteen. The fly tying started a few years later and, in Doug's words, "it became all consuming." Doug had an older friend who was a fly tier and he was happy to teach him the basics. Another friend gave him a vice, and Doug was soon tying flies that caught fish.

Doug believes in passing on what he knows to other fly tiers and has taught several fly-tying classes over the years. "When

"About the middle of May, the trout in all the lakes and rivers are in the most likely mood to take the fly. They are now gorged with the may fly (which is black in colour and otherwise quite unlike the English species) until they come to the very pink of condition. Every rock and brush at the edge of the sheltered lakes is now found on a fine, warm day to be fairly covered with these choice morsels of trout diet. At times the myriads of insects rise on the wing until they suggest a cloud of smoke."

Arthur P. Silver, *Farm-Cottage,
Camp and Canoe in Maritime Canada*
(1907)

Nepisiguit Grey

Tag:	Oval silver	Ribbing:	Oval silver tinsel
Tip:	Yellow silk floss	Throat:	Brown, collared and tied
Tail:	Golden pheasant crest		down
Butt:	Peacock herl	Wing:	Bronze mallard
Body:	Medium grey wool		

I started tying flies the old timers were very secretive about how they tied their flies," recalls Doug, "they wouldn't tell you a thing. Today new fly tiers have lots of books and videos available to them so it is much easier to start tying on your own if you have to." Doug believes it is important to tie with other people: "You always pick up a new technique or a simpler way of doing something when you sit down and tie flies with other fly tiers." He is also a firm believer that you cannot build a good fly if you start with inferior materials or tools.

Doug tied commercially for several years and now ties for himself and friends as well as custom orders and for charity. He believes you don't need to carry a lot of flies to be a successful salmon fisher: "If I had some Bombers and Bugs, Black Bear Green Butts and Butterflies I would have all the flies I need," laughs Doug. Like Henry Ford, he believes that any colour will do as long as it is black, "especially on the Miramichi." He sticks to black flies throughout much of the season except for black salmon fishing in the spring when he uses big streamers, or fall fishing when he uses flies like the General Practitioner or marabou winged flies. Doug had this to say on the latter:

"When I began tying flies. I was told that there were two patterns I had to have: the Bone Crusher and the Grasshopper. The Grasshopper was a good fly and I caught trout with it, but I never caught a fish on the Bone Crusher. Now, the pattern is a good one. It was created by Rev. L. E. Davis for landlocked salmon on the St. Croix River. However, I never had any luck with it and it became a running joke between myself and my friend Bill Ensor. We were fishing together at Flo's on the Miramichi a number of years ago and Bill hooked a big fish. The fishing was slow so I was anxious to see what Bill caught the fish on. When I tailed it I saw the fly was a Bone Crusher, tied on a 2/0 hook with about a 4X shank.... About ten years later on another fishing trip I was being skunked and Bill hooked eight fish. I tailed another fish and in its jaws was the very same fly; Ensor had kept that fly for ten years, waiting for the right moment."

Doug varies his "any fly as long as it is black" rule when he moves out of the Miramichi watershed. On the Restigouche, for example, where the water is clear, he uses silver or green flies. Doug doesn't like flies with too much material: "A sparse fly moves better in the water; it swings the right way and breathes or pulses and has a lot of movement while a heavily dressed pattern lacks that lifelike movement." Doug is a serious student of fly movement and how salmon react to the drift of a fly: "On the Kedgewick River there is a tower where you can climb up and watch the fish as anglers drift flies through the pool. There is a much different reaction to a fly fished right by their nose compared to one six feet above them on the surface." He has used viewing opportunities from bridges to rip rap and river banks to observe fly movement and the reaction of salmon.

While part of the appeal of fly fishing and fly tying to Doug is the constant experimentation with techniques and patterns, he also has strong feelings about new fly patterns and how some people approach their development. He feels that there enough flies out there, and that changing the colour of the butt or body of a fly and changing the wing material doesn't make a new pattern. Which is not to say he doesn't experiment with patterns for his own enjoyment. He'll change silver tinsel to gold for example, but doesn't feel it's necessary to give it a new name. Two of Doug's old-time favourites on New Brunswick rivers are the Nepisiguit Gray and the Black Fairy. "None of us can think like a fish and after all these years I still have no idea why a salmon takes a fly. I do think it is important to have faith in your fly. Ask me what my favourite fly is and I'll tell you it's the last one I caught a fish on. You need faith in your flies to carry you over the dry days."

Jacques Heroux

Jacques was born in Cabano, Quebec, in 1957. After attending the University of Moncton, he joined the New Brunswick Community College system, where he serves as a director of programming. As a boy of twelve, a neighbour taught him how to tie flies as well as fly fish for trout. He's returned to both activities in the past fifteen years, fly fishing for salmon in New Brunswick and tying flies again. A friend taught him how to tie hairwing salmon flies and he took a course on tying traditional featherwings from Bryant Freeman. Jacques credits Freeman, Jerome Molloy and Marc LeBlanc for making him the fly tier he is today. "They were very generous and never hesitated in sharing their experience and expertise with me."

Jacques began tying commercially a few years ago and is kept very busy selling flies through his website: www.salmosalar.info.ca. He also ties for a number of camps and shops in Quebec. Jacques's interest in fly tying led him to begin a fly-tying club in Dieppe about seven years ago. "Today we have fifty-five members. We meet every week during the winter, and last year we had four women and four teenagers join us." Jacques is also responsible for the annual Dieppe Fly Tying Forum, which has been held for the past two years.

His preference for fly-tying hooks is "the basics"—Mustad bronze down eye hooks such as the Mustad 3399A for bugs and butterflies, and the Medway hook for wet flies.

Same Thing Murray

Tag:	Fine oval silver tinsel	Wing:	A few strands of green Krystal Flash under moosehair, tied sparsely
Tail:	Orange hackle barbs		
Head:	Black ostrich herl, followed by black thread		
Body:	Rear two-thirds: green floss; front one-third: peacock herl	Hackle:	Black, tied as a collar and slanted rearward

Although he didn't develop it himself, the "Same Thing Murray" fly is the only one he felt worth bringing back from obscurity. In addition to dyeing his own flies, Jacques has also created a number of specialty flies which his corporate clients use both for fishing and as gifts to their clients.

According to Jacques, there are two types of flies: flies for fishermen and flies to catch fish. Asked what the difference is, Jacques says, "Fishing flies need to be sparse, not too heavily dressed." His flies have won awards at several international fly-tying contests and his traditional featherwing salmon fly he tied, the Lady Amherst, was featured on the Classic Salmon Fly poster from the ALS Society of Canada.

John Lyons

As one of the resident fly tiers in the W. W. Doak fly fishing store in Doaktown, John is well known for his mastery of spinning deer hair for bugs and bombers. He was born in 1970 in Doaktown and grew up fishing the local waters. "If you are born in Doaktown then you grow up with a fly rod in your hands," laughs John. His fly tying began at age twelve when he began tying with a friend from school. Later, he took a course at the salmon museum and from there bought a fly-tying kit from Jerry Doak at the store. John eventually began working part-time at W. W. Doak while he was still in school. He tied at home for a time, then in 1988 started full-time. He's been here ever since."

With Bruce tying hairwing flies, John turned to tying bugs and bombers. Their popularity means there's always a demand.

Tying the number of flies that he does, John has some firm ideas on materials and techniques: "I use deerhair exclusively, never caribou, and I like a hook with a wide gape. You need good hook exposure so the fish can be hooked. For the bugs I use a Mustad 3399A hook. I used to use the Mustad 38941 for bombers but they stopped making it so now I use our own W. W. Doak hooks."

John also had some suggestions regarding tools: "If you are tying any amount of deerhair flies then you need good scissors. Get ones with serrated blades; they will make a big difference. A ceramic bobbin also makes it easier to handle your thread. Good tools are important."

According to John, the Green Machine is a big seller at the shop, and the natural deer hair bomber with a white tail and brown or orange hackle is another favourite. "Adding a white tail seems to increase the effectiveness," says John, " even the Green Machine seems to fish better with a white calf tail."

Like Bruce Waugh and Jerry Doak, John is also an ardent angler, fishing mostly for trout. He enjoys fishing for sea trout on the Miramichi with small dry flies. The #10 Royal Wulff, he says, "is as good as any."

Orange River Shrimp

Tail:	Orange polar bear, extending a body length beyond the bend, a few strands of Krystal Flash on top is optional	Rib:	Small oval silver tinsel
Body:	Rear half: hot orange scintilla dubbing; front half: peacock herl	Wing:	Three lacquered golden pheasant tippets, the first tied in to reach the ends of the body, the second on top and reaching two-thirds of the way to the end of the body, the third to reach the one-third point
Hackle:	Orange, tied in by the tip at the rear and palmered forward, top barbules forced down		

Marc Madore

Marc was born in Larder Lake, Ontario, in 1942. He grew up sport fishing in the lakes and streams around Timmins before joining the Canadian Armed Forces in 1961. Marc tied his first fly, a Dark Montreal, in 1958 but it would be several years before he would start tying seriously. He took it up again when he was stationed in Germany in 1967, and took his first fly-tying course there. He hasn't stopped since.

Marc credits a well-known New Brunswick fly tier, the late Garnet Tweedie, with helping him become a better fly tier: "I met Garnet when I came to Gagetown for training. He was selling flies at that time and we became good friends. He was a very good fly tier and he taught me a lot about tying hairwing salmon flies." Marc retired from the military in 1995 and moved to Blackville, New Brunswick, where he began to tie flies commercially.

At one time he was tying over ten thousand flies a year, but has cut back in recent years. Active as a fly tier, Marc has also found time to teach fly tying. One of his students is Cathy Colford, who now ties commercially for Brock Curtis in his shop, Miramichi River Outfitters.

For Marc, action in the water is the most important thing in a salmon fly. Most anglers use flies that are too big, and Marc insists that a smaller fly catches more fish.

Marc created the Orange River Shrimp, one of his River Shrimp series. He was looking for an alternative to the shrimp imitations now available. He ties five colour variations: orange, light blue, yellow, green and black.

Marc's flies have been featured in a number of books, including *Modern Atlantic Salmon Flies* and *Shrimp and Spey Flies for Salmon and Steelhead*. He has created several unique patterns such as the Madoreabou Assassins, soft hackled flies which are effective on spring salmon.

Akroyd

Tag:	Gold oval tinsel
Tail:	Golden peasant crest, over which are five to ten golden pheasant tippett fibres, half as long as the crest.
Body:	In two equal parts: Rear half, yellow seal fur or substitute, palmered with yellow hackle. The rear section is ribbed with gold

oval tinsel. Front half: black floss ribbed with silver oval tinsel. The original was palmered with black heron but Jerome substitutes black bear tied at the throat.

Wing: Two narrow strips of white turkey, reaching to the tip of the tail and set low over the body.

Jerome Molloy

Jerome was born in St. John's, Newfoundland, in 1956 and lived there until he was nine years old. At that time he moved with his family to Prince Edward Island, where they lived until they moved to Saint John, New Brunswick. Jerome fished for trout with his father while they lived on PEI and can remember attempting to tie a fly after seeing some for sale in a local store. "I went home, pulled some feathers from a pillow and tried to tie them on a safety pin," laughs Jerome, "but I didn't catch any fish with it."

Jerome didn't begin fly fishing until he moved to Saint John and learned that there were salmon in the St. John River. A trip to the local library provided him with a copy of Helen Shaw's book *Fly Tying* and

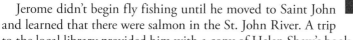

"Bryant Freeman jockeyed the green skiff across the current and dropped the killick above the rumble of Bear Falls. On the far side of the pool, Dick and Robbie were already stripping line from their reels, swishing salmon flies into the evening air. We were in business after a 700 mile trip by car and ferry from Westfield, Massachusetts, to the Medway River at Greenfield, Nova Scotia.

'Tie on that yellow fly,' Bryant said, 'and drift it past the boil there.'

The old favorites—Thunder and Lightning, Jock Scott, Durham Ranger, Silver Doctor and Dusty Miller—are all killers on the Medway, but in recent years squirrel tail flies have really hit the jackpot. I tied on the one Bryant suggested, a No. 6 hook dressed with a peacock herl body, golden pheasant tippet, squirrel tail wings and bright yellow hackle."

Ted Janes,
"Atlantics in Nova Scotia," *The Atlantic Salmon Journal*
(1957)

that got him started. Later he took a course from Saint John fly tier Warren Duncan; Jerome credits Warren with having a big influence on his fly tying.

Jerome read every book and magazine he could find on fly tying. One of the magazines he read featured flies tied by Bill Hunter of Hunter's Angling in New Boston, New Hampshire. He was so impressed, he eventually travelled to Bill Hunter's shop to attend a workshop on tying featherwing salmon flies. Jerome's fly tying progressed rapidly, and in 1990 he entered a world championship sponsored by the Federation of Quebec Salmon Associations (FQSA), where he won first place in both the featherwing, and hairwing Atlantic salmon fly categories. His featherwing fly was a Thunder and Lightning while the hairwing was an Orange Blossom. Jerome won the contest again in 1991, for his featherwing fly, a Childers.

Jerome's flies have long been in demand by anglers and he has tied commercially right from the beginning. Today he ties for clients around the world, and his flies are fished from New Brunswick to Russia.

These are flies that are meant to be fished, so he believes that durability is very important, and can only be achieved by using quality materials "right from the hook to the hackle."

He likes to use the Green Highlander and Jock Scott, but when the water is cold he uses the Akroyd, which he finds effective for salmon on the Margaree in the fall. As far as bugs and bombers go, after discovering Bryant Freeman's Carters Bug, he uses that exclusively. He likes it because it "looks natural, like a bug. With a dry fly I believe that the character of the fly is important, and the Carters Bug has a very buggy look to it." Jerome credits Bryant Freeman with teaching him a lot about flies and fishing. "Bryant is a natural fisherman. He is by far the best dry fly fisherman that I have ever seen."

Jerome's flies have been featured in Paul Marriner's *Modern Atlantic Salmon Flies* and Bob Verveka's book on spey flies. He was also profiled in Dewey Gillespie's *Fly Tyers of New Brunswick*. One of his flies, a Green Highlander, was featured on the poster of classic salmon flies produced by the ALS Society of Canada. He ties every day on his Regal vice and is in demand for his workshops on fly tying. Jerome believes that there are plenty of salmon patterns around and he seldom varies from established patterns. "I am a traditionalist at heart," he says, "and I like to tie using the materials listed for each pattern. But I will substitute rather than not tie a fly." An example is the Akroyd he tied for this book. While the original calls for heron hackle, Jerome substitutes black bear hair to make a fly

"One fall on the Miramichi, Perley Palmer, a respected old-time guide of those waters, slipped a #2 Mickey Finn into my hands with the words, 'This is an awfully good fly, and it will take them sometimes when nothing else seems to.' He was right. It took two salmon in short order."

Lee Wulff, *The Atlantic Salmon* (1958)

that not only looks like the original, but is also more durable. Jerome's choice of the Akroyd is interesting because when it was created by Charles Akroyd of Brora, Scotland, in 1878, he called it "The Poor Man's Jock Scott," which happens to be one of Jerome's favourite flies.

Abraham Lewis "Abe" Munn

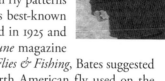

1858–1937

Abe Munn was born in Holtville, New Brunswick, and began fishing gaspereau commercially with his father as a boy. He later became a well-known guide and angler in the Boisetown area. While he favoured traditional featherwing salmon flies such as the Silver Doctor or Jock Scott, he also developed several fly patterns that are well known on the Miramichi. Perhaps his best-known pattern is the Abe Munn Killer, which he developed in 1925 and which was featured in John McDonald's 1948 *Fortune* magazine article, "The Atlantic Salmon." In *Atlantic Salmon Flies & Fishing*, Bates suggested that the fly appeared to be the earliest named North American fly used on the Miramichi River.

Abe Munn and his flies obviously had a significant influence on New Brunswick fly tying. Noted New Brunswick outfitter Jack Russell, who ran a salmon camp on the Miramichi, had this to say about Munn's flies: "There has been little change in the basic patterns of flies from the beginning of salmon fishing on this continent. I do not mean to imply that there have not been some changes, yet the standard patterns such as Jock Scott, Black Dose, Silver Gray, Dusty Miller, Silver Doctor, Durham Ranger, Mar Lodge, hold good year after year. In addition to that list there are many flies which seem to do well on different waters. On the Miramichi, for instance, we use the Abe Munn Killer during the summer. That fly was originated on the river by an old guide, who probably had to tie the original with barnyard feathers."

Father Elmer Smith

Father Smith was an Anglican minister who was born in Philadelphia, PA. He made his first fishing trip to the Miramichi in 1940 and soon became very interested in Atlantic salmon. He continually experimented with different types and sizes of salmon flies at various water levels. He was also a student of salmon behaviour, observing their reaction to a particular fly under various circumstances and keeping detailed records of his observations. An expert fly tier, he introduced several salmon patterns that continue to be an important part of the sport today.

Father Smith's life and flies have been dealt with in some detail by numerous authors in magazine articles and books on fly tying. New Brunswick author Michael Brislain's book *Bugging the Atlantic Salmon* is devoted to the topic of tying and fishing Father Smith's creations. The only exceptions to the rule that "everything is a variation of something that's been tied before," are Father Smith's Bugs and Bombers. Perhaps no other flies have made such an impact on fly fishing for Atlantic salmon. There are few salmon rivers in the world where they can't be found, either in their original style or as variations such as the Green Machine, Shady Lady and many more. They have also become a favourite fly for steelhead and trout.

Father Smith's display at the Atlantic Salmon Museum in Doaktown includes a short write-up on his life and work, and his role as a fly tier, teacher, and conservationist; it states, "He is best remembered as an ardent angler who spent many years on the river and one who preferred fishing during the early morning hours. But never on a Sunday."

Larry Tracy

Larry was born in Fredericton Junction, New Brunswick, in 1926 and lived there until 1945, when he joined the Canadian Pacific Railway and moved to Saint John. He later worked with the New Brunswick Telephone Company, retiring in 1990. Larry fished as a boy, often traveling by bicycle to fish local brooks for trout. He began fly tying while working with the CPR. "We used to have a layover at McAdam Junction and the conductor, Clarence Thomas, would tie flies in the caboose. He got me started," recalls Larry. "I have been at it ever since." Larry also took some fly-tying lessons from Warren Duncan and now does some teaching through the Hammond River Anglers Association.

Dick Stewart's *Universal Fly Tying Guide* is a favourite reference, as is Keith Fulsher's and Charles Krom's book on hairwing salmon flies.

Many anglers will be familiar with one of Larry's fly patterns, the LT Special. It is included in Paul Marriner's book *Modern Atlantic Salmon Flies* and is carried in the W. W. Doak catalogue. Larry explains its genesis: "I developed it for fishing the Cains River. Anglers were fishing the standard patterns such as the Mickey Finn, Copper Killer, Allie's shrimp, and so on. I decided to come up with a fly which combined most of the features of these flies. I wanted a fly which also combined all the colours of the leaves in the fall: red, yellow, green and orange. I used diamond braid for the body instead of copper tinsel and added a two-piece wing of orange and green bucktail. I finished it off with red and yellow hackle and an orange head. I've caught quite a few fish on it and it even caught fish in Russia."

LT Special

Tag:	Copper diamond braid and fluorescent orange floss	Hackle:	Two winds of yellow followed by two winds of wine, tied as a collar
Body:	Copper diamond braid	Head:	Fluorescent orange
Wing:	Orange bucktail under Kelly green bucktail with a few strands of copper Krystal Flash mixed in		

For hooks, Larry used to use a standard Mustad 36890 but now prefers the Medway hook sold by Bryant Freeman. He found the Mustad hooks always needed sharpening, whereas Bryant's are chemically sharpened.

Larry prefers a sparse fly for most of his salmon fishing. "On the Miramichi you don't want too big a fly, in my opinion. If you are fishing bigger water then you need a larger fly. When I fished the St. John, I used fully dressed flies."

Larry is also a fan of the bug and bomber and ties some of his bombers with antelope hair, which he says is a nice hair to work with and floats well.

Larry has also guided salmon anglers over the years, which he enjoyed. He used to tell them that a straight thirty-five-foot cast was better than a crooked sixty-five-foot one, because most of the time the inexperienced anglers were casting right over the fish.

Asked about his favourite patterns, Larry replies: "The Black Bear green butt is always a good choice, and my own pattern, the LT Special. I like a fly with a multiple-colour butt. In my experience, a fly with a red and green butt will out-fish a fly with a single-colour butt every day. In the fall, red and orange flies are a good choice. The old-time guides liked to use gaudy flies for fall fishing. One of their favourite patterns was the Chief Needabah streamer. It is still a good fly, both in the fall and in the spring."

Larry has sold a few flies over the years but he doesn't consider himself a commercial tier. He can often be found fishing with two other well-known New Brunswick fly tiers, Bryant Freeman and Jerome Molloy.

Bruce Waugh

Bruce was born in 1965 in Sussex, New Brunswick, and later moved with his family to Nova Scotia, then to Doaktown. He is well known to anglers who drop into W. W. Doak's store as one of the in-house fly tiers, along with Jerry Doak and John Lyons. He started tying flies shortly after moving to Doaktown in 1980. "I was in grade nine at the time and Jerry taught me the basics. I began tying for the store the next year and have been at it ever since," he says.

"Two miles above Bruin farm and twelve miles from the Forks, Bedell Brook, with its dead water, attracts the sportsman. Here…are found the largest brook trout on Miramichi. Seven and eight pound fish are said to be taken here. Three and a half is the largest I have seen; while the event of the trip was a double, hooked at a single cast of a parmachene belle and a squirrel tail. The two weighed respectively two and three-quarters and two and a half pounds."

Tappan Adney,
Summer Days on the Miramichi
(1902)

Bruce ties most of the wet salmon flies for the store, averaging about fifteen thousand flies in around two hundred different patterns each year. He learned most of what he knows from Jerry, but doesn't discount what he's learned from customers—one of the advantages of tying in the shop. "They tell you what is taking fish or not."

According to Bruce, durability is important, but second to consistency: "If someone bought one of my Cossebooms last season and comes in to buy one this year they should be able to buy the identical fly."

Maintaining consistency when tying commercially means balancing speed with quality. "Speed shouldn't compromise fly quality or consistency," says Bruce.

The Black Bear Green Butt and the Undertaker are Bruce's most popular wet flies, especially on the Miramichi. In "dries," the Bomber is number one. Bruce notes that in the last twenty-five years he has seen some changes in what anglers buy for flies, with smaller flies, #8 and #10, more common.

Like John and Jerry, Bruce ties on Regal vices, which he calls "a real workhorse of a vice. I tie up to fifteen thousand flies a year and every couple of years or so I may have to replace the jaws. They are a great vice."

Bruce continues in the tradition developed by Wally and Jerry Doak to tie existing patterns and avoid developing new ones. "There are enough patterns now," he says. "Really, there are no new flies. Everything is usually a variation of something else. For instance the Butterfly is a variation of the Coachman, and so on. There are very few flies which are new and innovative. One of the few which comes to mind is the Bomber. It was completely different from popular dry flies of the day and, most importantly, it caught fish."

3

Fly Tiers
of Newfoundland and Labrador

"There is no country so near England at the present hour which offers so many attractions to the sportsman as Newfoundland.[...] Newfoundland is no bad substitute for Norway. The beauty of the bold and deeply indented coast; the excellence of the fishing amid the wild solitudes; the countless number of lakes and streams by which the island is watered—all conspire to make of Newfoundland a veritable paradise of the angler for trout and salmon."

Arthur Silver,
"The Sea-Trout and Salmon Streams of Newfoundland,"
in Farm-Cottage, Camp and Canoe in Maritime Canada
(1907)

Newfoundland and Labrador offer anglers some of the best sport-fishing opportunities in North America. There is no question that Atlantic salmon is king in the province. There are 177 rivers listed or scheduled for fly fishing only for Atlantic salmon.

On the island of Newfoundland, salmon begin nosing in from the cold North Atlantic in late May or early June, fat from feeding on schools of capelin. Salmon runs continue through the early summer, often triggered by rises of water following rain storms. In Labrador runs are generally later, running into July and August. Some years heavy pack ice can further delay the entry of fish to their home rivers.

There are likely more fly-fishing anglers and fly tiers in Newfoundland and Labrador than anywhere else in North America. Traditional salmon flies such as the Blue Charm and Thunder and Lightning continue to be popular in the province; however, the tiers on the island are also among the most innovative and creative in the world. Using local materials such as hair from moose and caribou, they craft flies such as the Silver Tip and Orange Caribou Bug, which are deadly on local salmon rivers.

Most Newfoundland rivers are small and easily waded. There are some big rivers, however, and the Humber, which runs into the sea near Corner Brook, has long been known as the home of big multi-sea winter salmon. But not all of Newfoundland and Labrador's salmon run to sea. The province also supports good fishing for landlocked Atlantic salmon, or as they are known locally, ouananiche. Ouananiche on the island seldom reach large sizes and a one-kilogram fish is considered a good one. However, in Labrador fish weighing up to ten kilograms are occasionally caught. While ouananiche will rise for dry flies, most anglers have better luck fishing big streamers.

In a province where the term "Old Trout" is a term of endearment, it is no surprise that trout fishing is also an important part of life in Newfoundland and Labrador. Brook or speckled trout is the only native trout species found on the island, while lake trout and arctic char are also found on Labrador. Brook trout abound in the thousands of ponds that dot the island, but many are small and stunted because of limited forage available to them coupled with a short growing season. However, many rivers support runs of sea trout that take advantage of more plentiful feeding opportunities in bays and estuaries by leaving freshwater and running to the sea. These fish return in early summer and provide great sport on the fly.

Many anglers consider the trout fishing in Labrador to be the best in the world. The Minipi and Eagle river systems regularly produce large brook trout of up to four kilograms. Brown and rainbow trout have also been introduced to the province. The brown trout was introduced to rivers on the Avalon Peninsula, where it has prospered. As is the case everywhere, brown trout on Newfoundland can be frustratingly difficult to catch. Local anglers often have success using small nymphs and wet flies as small as size 16 to 18. First brought to Newfoundland by angling clubs at the end of the nineteenth century, rainbow trout are found in several ponds near St. John's on the Avalon Peninsula.

Harold "Smokey" Ball

Smokey was born in Deer Lake in 1935. He still lives there with his wife and when he isn't busy tying flies, he also serves as the town's mayor. Smokey worked as a heavy equipment operator until a heart condition forced him to retire in 1983. It was while he was home recuperating from open heart surgery that he began tying flies. He was finding the time long and a cousin, Dan Ball, suggested he start tying flies to pass the time. He brought along a vice for Smokey and the two of them began tying. His cousin started him tying bugs and Smokey obviously took to it as he is still tying them today. In fact the only flies he ties are bugs and bombers.

Smokey's flies are tight and well proportioned—and popular. Many anglers in Newfoundland and Labrador wouldn't go on the water without a selection of Smokey's bugs in their fly box. Ches Loughlin featured Smokey in the 1987 *SPAWNER* magazine and his fame continues to spread.

Smokey's Bug

Tail:	White calftail	Hackle:	Various colours
Body:	Caribou hair, natural or dyed, spun on and trimmed	Wing:	White calf tail

A good bug, according to Smokey, is "one that doesn't come apart." Smokey ties all his flies with caribou hair and finds that it floats much better than deer hair. He also packs the hair very tightly and trims the bottom of every fly flat so it floats right on the water surface. He ties his bombers in a range of three sizes, #4, #6 and #8 on Mustad 9672 hooks. While Smokey's biggest seller is the classic Orange Bug tied with a white calftail, natural caribou body, orange hackle, and white wing, he also experiments with various colour combinations. "Last year a black-bodied bomber with white calftail and orange hackle worked great," Smokey says "and on the Castors a white-bodied bomber with blue hackle was good."

An active fly tier, Smokey is also an avid angler and has been since he was a boy. He caught his first salmon at Cache Rapids on the Humber River when he was twelve and has been fishing ever since. In recent years he bought a camper and covers the salmon rivers of the west coast of Newfoundland as well as southern Labrador. However, he still finds the best salmon fishing is on his doorstep at the Tail Race in Deer Lake. "It's the best salmon hole in the world," he states.

Art Barnes

1900–1994

Art Barnes was a well-known figure on the Lower Humber River, fondly remembered by those who knew him as a real sportsman and a great angler. Three of his sons-in-law, Ches Loughlin, Bud Cook and Reg Nichols, are all well-known anglers in their own right and they all speak highly of their late father-in-law. "Art knew how to catch the big fish," Ches says. "Every year he would get his picture in the paper with a big fish or two of up to thirty pounds."

Reg remembers Art as someone who got great enjoyment from the outdoors, whether hunting or fishing, "and it made no difference to him if he was successful or not. It was a bonus if he caught a fish or a rabbit."

Art tied his own flies until his last year of fishing. He had a few patterns he liked: the Thunder and Lightning, Black Cosseboom, Dutot Blue Charm and the Orange Puppy. According to Ches, Art usually used a riffling hitch when fishing his flies. "He loved to fish and during the season he would be on the river every day except Sunday and when he fished he would spend time at each pool." To hook the bigger fish better, he frequently altered his fly hooks by opening up the gape with a pair of pliers, a technique also used by Waldo Hendsbee in Nova Scotia.

Art kept a boat on the Lower Humber and Reg often went with him to Boom Siding. Both Reg and Paul Barnes, Art's son, recall how superstitious Art was about his fishing. You had to turn the boat clockwise with the sun, for example. "Sometimes I would pretend I was turning against the sun and he would holler at me," laughs Reg. "He also believed that the salmon always run up the river with their left eye to the river bank so he would always fish on that side."

Reg corroborates Ches's recollection of their father-in-law's fly preferences: "Art liked the Thunder and Lightning, a #6 on a double hook, early in the season. Later he became a fan of the Orange Puppy. He was a real gentleman. I often saw him hook a fish and pass the rod to a young fellow to play it. It made no difference to him if he lost the fish or not."

"He was the King of the Humber," says Bud Cook. "Most people fished the upper part of the river because there were a lot of grilse up there but Art liked to fish for the big fish in the lower part of the river. They were harder to catch and there were probably only half a dozen anglers who regularly fished there." Bud told me that Art fished right up until he was ninety years old. "Reg put a chair in the boat for him so he could fish. The last year he fished he caught seven grilse."

Fred Clarke

1910–1978

Well known as an angler and fly tier in the Corner Brook area, Fred Clarke played an important role in publicizing the sport-fishing opportunities available in Newfoundland and Labrador. He formed the Bay of Islands Rod and Gun Club in 1948 and served as its first president. The Club played an important role in teaching fly tying to anglers in the Corner Brook area for many years. He also operated the Angler's Mart, a Corner Brook sporting goods store specializing in fly-tying and fishing equipment.

Fred Clarke fished widely throughout Newfoundland and Labrador, at one time employing two guides. Many of the rivers he regularly fished could only be reached at that time by coastal boat. He often hosted outdoor magazine writers to showcase the salmon and trout fishing available. Corey Ford, a writer for *Field and Stream*, detailed a fishing trip he made to the Lower Humber in the February 1954 issue of the magazine. In the story Ford wrote about the success he had catching a large Lower Humber salmon on a fly that Clarke was involved in developing with well-known fly tier Max Rabbitts and Dr. R. F. Dove. The fly was the Chimo and in the story Corey Ford explains how it received its name:

"Hedley turned the slab of salmon grilling before the fire, and a rich oily odor filed the room. I re-examined the bedraggled fly that had taken the fish. 'Why is this called the Chimo?' I asked Dr. Dove curiously. 'It's the name of my camp here,' he answered. 'It's an Eskimo word meaning welcome. I first heard it years ago up in Baffin Land. There's a settlement in northern Quebec on Ungava Bay named Fort Chimo.'"

The Chimo

Tag:	Silver tinsel	Ribs:	5 turns oval gold tinsel
Body:	Dubbed seal fur, rear one-third orange and front two-thirds black teased out	Wing:	Black moose
		Cheeks:	Blue chatterer

In a later article, Clarke brags that the Chimo had been responsible for "the downfall of many good salmon from Humber pools."

Clarke's Chimo fly was very popular on the Humber River during the 1950s and '60s, but gradually was replaced with new patterns. It was well-known Corner Brook fly tier Rob Solo who rediscovered the Chimo and helped to bring it to the light in an article he wrote for the 1998 issue of *SPAWNER* magazine. Orange and black make a great colour combination for the big fish of the Lower Humber, says Rob, and his success with the few Chimo flies he has tied mean that the pattern has a permanent place in his fly box.

Ian Gall

Ian was born in 1939 in Dundee, Scotland, and moved to Canada in 1968. He sailed with the British Merchant Navy and joined the Canadian Coast Guard when he came to Canada. He lived in Dartmouth, Nova Scotia, from 1968 until 1974, when he moved to St. John's, his current home. He writes articles on fly fishing and fly tying for *SPAWN-ER* magazine.

Ian remembers fishing flounder in Scotland as a boy and has been fishing ever since. His fly tying began when he was eleven. He joined the local angling club and they offered fly-tying lessons to members once a week over the winter. When he moved to Nova Scotia, Ian took fly-tying courses from Ron Alcott and Mike Crosby. He is also an avid reader of anything on fly tying and fly fishing.

Ian is a keen observer of what is happening on the water when he is fishing, and he uses that information to aid him with his fly tying. As an example, Ian related an experience he had when fishing for sea run trout on the Musquodoboit River in Nova Scotia. Ian was standing on the edge of the river fishing and saw hundreds of small eels swimming along the edge of the river. These were larval or glass eels entering the river after their long migration from the Sargasso Sea near Bermuda. Once they were in the river for a short period of time, these eels would take on the dark pigmentation found in older eels. Ian reasoned that the trout would be taking advantage of this ample supply of feed, so he went home and came up with an elver fly that consisted of a white thread body and pale blue ostrich herl, four or five strands, to which he added an eye. "The trout loved it," Ian laughs, "although the herl didn't hold up that well. The trout's teeth used to tear it up." Ian also tied the same fly with black ostrich herl to imitate young eels later in the season.

Peacock Olive Nymph

Tail:	A few fibres of a dark olive hen feather	Hackle:	Dark olive hen feather
Body:	Medium peacock olive chenille	Wing:	Mallard or teal breast feather; brown turkey wing feather is also good
Thorax:	Olive or black Antron, hare mask or seal fur		

Ian believes that sparseness is the most critical factor in tying a taking pattern for trout or salmon. He uses the example of a fly that he calls the Forteau MacIntosh. Ian ties the fly in the MacIntosh style on a #8-14 hook with no body, six red squirrel tail fibres, and one or two turns of hackle.

Although he uses moose hair for wings on some of his flies, Ian favours black squirrel tail for most of the wings on his salmon flies.

The Silver Tip is one of his first choices for salmon, followed by the Cosseboom. He fishes the Silver Tip in small sizes and uses uni-yarn as a body. He ties Cossebooms with an olive or green body and adds an underwing of floss topped by gray squirrel. Ian's favourite dry fly for salmon is a Chartreuse Bug with light green hackle and white calf tail wings.

Ian does some commercial fly tying for friends and custom orders, and is also actively involved in teaching fly-fishing and fly-tying classes each winter in St. John's.

While Ian is an avid salmon angler, he also gets a great deal of enjoyment from fishing trout. "Living on the Avalon Peninsula I have access to brook, brown and rainbow trout fishing within a short drive of my home. Brown trout are probably my favourite," Ian acknowledges. "They are very hard to catch." Ian's trout fishing begins on the, Waterford River which runs through St. John's, when the season opens mid-winter. Early-season angling is with nymphs or streamers and can be challenging fishing. Ian has had success with a Peacock Nymph he developed.

Ian believes white wing flies do well on Newfoundland rivers because they stand out in the dark water.

Don Hustins

Don was born in St. John's in 1946 and lives there today. He is retired from the provincial government, where he served as Director of Parks and Natural Areas for Newfoundland and Labrador. Don began fishing with his father, Gordon, when he was three or four years old. His father was an avid angler, and they fished for trout in the ponds and streams around St. John's. Don began salmon fishing when he was eight years old, accompanying his father to rivers of the Avalon Peninsula, including the Salmonier, Biscay Bay and Trepassey rivers. His fly-tying career began a few years later when he was thirteen and in the air cadets. As Don recalls, the cadets offered two courses, one on building model airplanes and another on fly tying. His father urged him to take the fly-tying course and Don hasn't stopped tying since.

The class, taught by Bill Vail, gave students basic tying techniques for standard trout flies. Don began tying to supply his father with trout and salmon flies. They worked well and his father's friends soon had Don tying for them as well. At that time Wulff flies were becoming popular, and Don was receiving requests to tie them. He was having problems setting the wings, and although the flies caught fish, he wanted to perfect his technique. His opportunity came during a family trip to the West Coast when he was seventeen or eighteen. Don and his father were fishing the Humber and in a conversation with another angler, Don mentioned his problems with the Wulff flies. The angler turned out to be a friend of Max Rabbitts, well-known fly tier in Corner Brook, and he arranged for Don to attend a fly-tying class with him.

Don also attended Ron Alcott's workshops in St. John's on tying featherwing salmon flies.

Don has tied commercially for over thirty years—tying helped to finance his university education—and he continues to tie commercially today, although he now laughs when he recalls some of his early commercial efforts. When he was sixteen, the government opened a moose hunt on the Avalon Peninsula for the first time. Don saw this as an opportunity to get some moose hair for his business so he placed an ad in the local paper saying that he wanted to buy moose hair for tying flies. He was deluged with calls from hunters willing to sell him moose hides, and as Don remembers, they were not too happy when he told them he wanted only one hide. The ad had an unexpected benefit, however: It prompted a call from an elderly lady who asked Don if he would be interested in purchasing her late husband's fly-tying equipment and supplies. Don purchased the lot and he is still using some of the material.

When Don began selling commercially, he was mostly tying "the standards," like the Silver Tip, Green Highlander and Blue Charm, in #6 or #8 with moosehair wings.

Don went to the University of New Brunswick in 1966 to do his forestry degree, and in September he went salmon fishing with a friend on the Nashwack River. It was the first time Don had seen the deerhair bug and the fact that his friend caught two salmon on it convinced him of its effectiveness. He soon on had his father send his fishing and fly-tying gear to New Brunswick. For the next several years Don sent bugs home to his father and they had success with them on Newfoundland rivers. Don's appreciation of the bug continues today—it's his favourite fly for trout and salmon, and he ties it from #2 to #14.

Green Highlander

Tag:	Flat silver		Body:	First two-thirds yellow floss; final one-third green floss
Butt:	Yellow floss			
Tail:	Golden pheasant, black ostrich		Throat:	Green hackle wound three times and overlain with yellow hackle fibres
Wing:	Brown squirrel tail			
Rib:	Oval silver tinsel			

Don notes that Leonard's book, *Flies*, and Herter's fly tying manual have both been aids to his fly tying.

Don ties on a Thompson vice and has no strong preference regarding fly hooks; he ties salmon flies on Mustad 36890 and bugs on Mustad 9672 hooks.

Don is constantly experimenting with new flies and techniques. He once tied a fly with only a few hairs from red squirrel tail and caught fish. "Fresh run salmon are in a taking mood," says Don, "so they will often bite anything. Once they have been in the river for a while, they are more fussy."

Today Don ties most of his salmon flies with squirrel or calf tail hair in the wings.

Don is a big fan of brown trout and he actively pursues them on the waters of the Avalon Peninsula. Sea run browns are found in several rivers and Don has seen them caught up to twenty pounds.

Don is presently writing a book on brown trout in Newfoundland and hopes to have it published shortly. It will outline the history of the species in Newfoundland as well as how, and where, to fish them.

Don Hutchens

Don was born in 1946 in Iowa. His father had come to Newfoundland during World War Two and met and married Don's mother, who was from Mount Pearl. The family returned to St. John's where Don grew up. He received his engineering degree from the Technical University of Nova Scotia and worked as an engineer with Newfoundland Telephone, retiring in 2001.

Don didn't begin salmon fishing until 1991 and began fly tying in 1997, by taking a fly-tying course with Ian Gall after receiving a fly-tying kit as a Christmas gift. He enjoyed it so much that he took the course two or three times. He graduated to the advanced course and recently won a silver medal in a fly-tying competition.

He credits *SPAWNER* magazine with inspiring him to develop his fly tying. He is especially interested in flies developed by Newfoundland fly tiers or by fly tiers from elsewhere who had success with a pattern in Newfoundland and Labrador.

Don has catalogued 394 flies that appeared in *SPAWNER* from 1979 until 2001. He developed a spreadsheet with information on the fly, the issue it appeared in (including a page reference), the area and river where it was fished, and its originator. He also has an impressive collection of flies he has tied—to date, 180 of the 398 patterns listed in *SPAWNER*. "I have lots of work ahead of me yet," he laughs.

Don credits a cable television show from Corner Brook as being a major influence on his early fly tying. The show was *Hooks and Hackle*, hosted by well-known Corner Brook fly tier Rob Solo.

In Don's opinion, each region in Newfoundland has its own unique fly-tying style. "For example," Don says, "in central Newfoundland, on rivers such as the Gander and Exploits, the guides do not like floating flies and they never use the riffling hitch. They like a sparse fly and will often clip off excess material if they think a fly is tied too full. On the West Coast of Newfoundland, salmon flies tied as streamers are very popular but they are not as popular on the Avalon or in central Newfoundland."

Don ties on a Regal. He tries to get salmon fishing for at least twenty days every season, and makes trips to the West Coast, Northern Peninsula and Central Newfoundland. While he uses a variety of fly patterns, Don feels that it is hard to argue with the success of the big Deerhair Bomber on Newfoundland rivers. In low water Don uses small flies, #10-14, and two of his most effective patterns are a white-winged Blue Charm or an Ingalls Butterfly.

Don believes that one of the attractions of fly tying is that you are always learning and you never have all the answers. As an example, he points to the 394 fly patterns that have appeared in *SPAWNER*. "All these flies have caught fish," he says. "It shows that salmon will probably take any fly, if conditions are right. However there are threads of commonality that run through successful patterns. Most successful flies leave a wake; the Orange Puppy, for example, makes a wake when fished. Rob Solo uses deerhair instead of hackle to get the same effect. The riffling hitch is the extreme form of this as it makes quite a disturbance in the water as the fly swings across the current."

Fly tying and fishing are an important part of Don's life and have become a second career for him. He is working on a book on the history of Newfoundland fly tiers and their patterns and also operates a tackle and fly-tying material business as well as doing some guiding.

Don Ivany

Don Ivany was born in 1960 in Corner Brook, and today lives with his family near the city in Irish Town. Don grew up fishing for trout and salmon with his father and caught his first salmon when he was nine years old on a Green Highlander at the Brook Pool on the Humber.

Don began fly tying in the late 1970s while working for Lundrigan's Construction in Corner Brook. One of the foremen there, Vick Russell, tied flies and showed Don the basics.

Don soon became involved in Atlantic salmon conservation work, a job he continues to this day. He became involved with the Salmon Preservation Association for the Waters of Newfoundland and with Parks Canada, where he served as an assistant fisheries biologist at Gros Morne National Park. While at Parks Canada, Don helped carry out fish stock assessment work on

Donnie's Black Fly

Tip:	Green fluorescent yarn; make it prominent	Wing:	Brown squirrel tail
Body:	Black wool yarn	Hackle:	Three winds of yellow hackle collared
Rib:	Oval gold tinsel		

Park rivers through operating counting fences and electro-fishing, among other methods. Don also spent time as a fisheries technician with the Department of Fisheries and Oceans before joining the Atlantic Salmon Federation in 1992, where he still works as the regional coordinator for Newfoundland and Labrador.

Don continues to be an avid angler and fly tier. I asked him if he had any favourite rivers for salmon in the province. "Oh, I would have to say the Castors and Sops Arm are two of my favourites," he replied.

Don helped begin a fly-tying club in Corner Brook in the early 1990s and is pleased with the number of young fly tiers in the area who came through the club.

Don's favourite fly pattern is the Green Cosseboom, and for dry flies he likes Smokey Ball's bombers, the natural with orange hackle. For his own tying, Don likes to experiment with patterns.

The fly that Don selected for the book resulted from his experiments in taking something from a few fly patterns, such as the Black Cosseboom and the Black Bear Green Butt, and combining them into one pattern. His father always referred to it as Donnie's Black Fly, and the name stuck.

Like many Newfoundland fly tiers, Don likes to tie on streamer hooks for his salmon flies. He believes that anything that shows up better seems to work. "For example, lately a lot of anglers have been having success tying flies such as the Blue Charm or Thunder and Lightning with a white wing. The flies seem to fish a lot better than with the traditional dark-coloured wing," he says.

Don varies his fly patterns and presentation with the season and fishing area. When fish have just entered the river, he likes to use silver- or green-bodied flies. When they have been moved up river, he switches to darker flies with black bodies such as the Blue Charm or his pattern. Don is also a big fan of the riffling hitch.

Don tends to concentrate mainly on salmon fishing these days, but he occasionally fishes for trout, and says that almost any small brown or black fly works well for trout.

Don favours caribou hair for his bugs and bombers, and finds that caribou hair floats much better than deerhair. He ties a simple bomber using natural caribou hair with orange hackle and white calf tail, fore and aft.

Don likes to keep his fishing simple. "In the rivers of Newfoundland and Labrador I mainly use a leader of eight-pound test Maxima early in the season. Sometimes I add a piece of six-pound for a tippet when the water drops. In the early part of the season you should use a big fly but later on you need to use small, sparse flies. I've seen anglers flail away at a fish after raising it. If you rest a fish for awhile and then fish over it with the original fly or something different, you will often be successful."

Ches Loughlin

Well known as an angler and fly tier, Ches Loughlin is also familiar to thousands of anglers as the long-time editor of *SPAWNER* magazine. Ches was born in

Howley on the shore of Newfoundland's Grand Lake in 1930. Some of his earliest memories are of his father carrying him on his shoulders as they went trout fishing. Grand Lake was known for its big trout, so Ches and his brother Jim spent many days fishing. Their fly tying began after reading some stories in the *Star Weekly* that included tips on how to tie flies. They plucked a few feathers from their Rhode Island Red rooster and wound them on the hook to make simple flies to catch trout. "Jim was my vice," laughs Ches. "He used to hold the hook in his fingers while I wound on the hackle."

Ches moved to Corner Brook when he was eighteen years old and began working for the Bank of Montreal, a career that lasted thirty-eight years. He also started fishing in Corner Brook. Fortunately for him, one of the tellers at the bank, Jean Cook, was married to Max Rabbitts, the well-known fly tier. At that time Max was selling featherwing salmon flies such as the Jock Scott for fifty cents apiece, and Ches used to buy half a dozen a week. Max often included a hairwing fly such as a Blue Charm along with the featherwings.

Harry's River was Ches's favourite spot. "I didn't have much equipment, no chest waders, no vest. I used a telescoping steel rod and a King Eider fly line that required constant dressing."

The popular fly patterns when Ches started salmon fishing were Wulff flies. Lee Wulff had introduced them to Max, who showed Ches how to tie them.

"Max was a good teacher," Ches says. "He was strict. If you didn't get it right he would have you take it apart and help you tie it the correct way." People were mostly tying moosehair flies, "even though Max was a big fan of English flies. No one bothered with the featherwings since they could catch as many fish with simpler patterns."

The first deerhair bomber fly Ches saw was fished by a New Brunswick angler named Fraser in the 1960s. The fly was tied with natural deer hair palmered with fiery brown hackle. When local tiers duplicated the pattern, they substituted orange hackle instead and found the fly fished even better.

Ches enjoys experimenting with flies and fly patterns, especially streamers, and listed the successful streamer fly Yellow Killer in the "deadly dozen" series of flies in the first issue of *SPAWNER* magazine. I asked him how his interest in fishing streamers for salmon developed. He laughed, "my brother-in-law, Paul Barnes, used to bring in some cards of flies from Japan for their store, Barnes Sporting Goods. They weren't fancy flies but there was one particular fly that one angler always came in and bought off the card. It was a streamer fly with hackle wings, two white ones in the centre and two yellow on the outside. Paul told me that this fellow was having luck with the pattern so I tried tying it with yellow monga tail as a wing. We had great luck with it and Bud Cook, another brother-in-law, christened it the Yellow Killer. He still swears by it."

Ches continues to experiment with new streamer patterns. One of his latest is the Humber Magic, which he featured in the 2001 issue of *SPAWNER*. "I tied it with some fluorescent material that Eric Baylis from Nova Scotia gave me. It was a sneaker lace but the colour, for some reason, really made an effective fly."

Ches mostly uses Mustad hooks for his flies—the 79580 for larger flies and the 9672 or 9671 for smaller flies. He mostly uses smaller flies for his fishing, often using size 10 or 12 streamers when fishing the Humber, where he does most of his fishing these days.

Ches believes the present state of fly tying on the island is very good. He stresses that fly tiers in Corner Brook are more fortunate than anglers in other areas: "The Humber is a great laboratory for testing new patterns," he says. "There are lots of fish, so you have plenty of opportunities to experiment with different flies, while anglers on the mainland, where there are fewer fish, may want to stick with tried and true flies."

Rick Maddigan

Rick was born in St. John's in 1951 and lives there with his family. When he is not busy teaching in the psychology department at Memorial University, he is likely at his fly-tying desk, or if the fishing season is open, on the bank of his favourite trout or salmon stream. Rick began fishing when he was four or five years old, and his fly tying began in his early teens. Rick's father, who first took Rick fishing, worked at Air Canada—as did Bas Vokey, a well-known St. John's fly tier. Rick met Bas through his father and began to learn how to tie flies from him.

Rick began tying flies commercially for Bas and helped finance his way through university by tying flies at three to four dollars a dozen. Bas supplied Rick with the materials, and Rick supplied the labour. He was tying mostly moosehair wet flies. The most popular patterns were the Blue Charm, Jock Scott and Silver Grey.

Rick's commercial fly-tying career ended when he finished his undergraduate degree. Today he ties for himself or friends and also donates flies to salmon conservation groups. He believes that the elements of a taking fly depend on conditions: "You need a variety of patterns, in various sizes, to meet different conditions on the river. Something different is often the key, especially if fish are seeing the same patterns every day. Look at the use of white flies, for example. Bas Vokey introduced the Polar White and it was an effective fly. At that time on the Salmonier River, black moosehair wings were popular. I substituted white moosehair on some flies I was tying, since I didn't have any polar bear, and it improved the fly." Rick also believes that presentation is important.

Rick likes turned-down eye bronze hooks for his salmon flies, and his favourite wet fly for salmon, his Salmonier Special, was featured in the *Atlantic Salmon Journal*.

Salmonier Special

Tag:	Flat gold tinsel	Rib:	Flat Gold tinsel
Body:	Claret wool	Wing:	White moose

Rick ties mostly during the winter, reserving the summer for fishing and family, and he would like to tie commercially again when he retires. He believes the current level of interest in fly tying in St. John's is alive and well. "The Salmonid Association for Eastern Newfoundland (SAEN) holds fly-tying socials twice a month during the winter as well as offering classes. Each social attracts fifteen to twenty fly tiers of varying skill levels. There is a lot of experience and knowledge at each social and the more experienced people are always happy to help out new tiers," he says.

While Rick does a lot of salmon fishing, he also enjoys trout fishing. His favourite trout flies are traditional wet flies, a Dark Montreal and Parmachene Belle. For sea trout he prefers a Mickey Finn with jungle cock eyes. In addition to the enjoyment he gets from tying his own flies, Rick ties his own in order to get what he wants in a fly. Sparseness is important to him; so is the special feeling of catching a fish on a fly he tied himself.

Besides being an accomplished fly tier, Rick has also written extensively on fly fishing and fly tying and his work has appeared in *SPAWNER* as well as the *Atlantic Salmon Journal*.

Reg Nichols

Born in 1929 in Deer Lake, Reg moved to Corner Brook in the 1950s to work as a mechanic in the Corner Brook Paper Mill, retiring in 1968. He fished trout when he lived in Deer Lake and was introduced to salmon fishing by his father-in-law, Art Barnes, and brother-in-law, Ches Loughlin. Reg began tying flies in the late 1950s under Ches's instruction. The first flies he tied were White and Grey Wulffs. It wasn't long before he began experimenting with variations of popular patterns. Reg remembers tying a White Wulff with one wing instead of the divided wing, calling it the Unicorn.

As he spent more time fishing and fly tying, Reg's flies became scantier and scantier. One of his favourites was a fly with a short brown hackle tail, peacock herl body, and a couple of winds of badger hackle, no wing. He also tied the fly with black hackle tail, ostrich herl body and a grey hackle. He never gave the pattern a name, but it was very successful for him on Harry's River. He fished the fly as a dry, and since it floated low in the water it was very hard to see.

Several books were helpful to Reg as a fly tier, including Joe Bates's *Atlantic Salmon Flies and Fishing* and Lee Wulff's book *The Atlantic Salmon*. But Reg also picked up a lot from talking to other anglers on the river, comparing and exchanging fly patterns.

Reg remembers that during the 1970s local fly tiers were experimenting with a lot of different flies for salmon, and Reg began tying salmon flies on streamer hooks. Reg's creation, the Orange Puppy, began to develop during this period: "It began with the ribbing," recalls Reg. "The Black Cosseboom I tied had a rib of embossed silver but the fish just tore it off and it seemed to fish as well without it so I left it

Orange Puppy

Tag:	Embossed flat silver	Body:	Black chenille
Tail:	Orange hackle very sparse	Wing:	Grey squirrel tail
		Throat:	Orange hackle
Butt:	Fluorescent green chenille	Collar:	Orange chenille

off. I also replaced the yellow hackle with orange and it also seemed to increase its effectiveness." Reg trimmed the hackle to form a ball at the head but later switched to orange chenille instead of hackle because it held up better. The Orange Puppy was born. The first time Reg fished the fly was at Big Falls on the Humber River. He was guiding some family members and tied up a few flies in his trailer. The fly immediately began to catch fish, some days when the fish wouldn't look at other flies.

The fly didn't have a name until Reg's nephews christened it the Orange Killer; it became the Orange Puppy when his brother-in-law Ches Loughlin asked him for a pattern for the first *SPAWNER* magazine in 1979. "I decided to call it the Orange Puppy. I figured that it was a pup or a grand pup of the Cosseboom," laughs Reg.

Reg generally uses Mustad 9671 and 9272 hooks for his salmon flies. Early in the season and during high water, he favours #4s, but the remainder of the season most of his flies will be #6.

His favourite salmon flies are the Orange Puppy, the Cosseboom, and Green Highlander.

Reg now ties several variations of the Puppy, adding a fluorescent green butt, different body colours and some orange Krystal Flash for a tail—just a few strands, and only in the tail, not in the wing. He likes to tie his flies sparse, believing that they fish better than a fully dressed fly.

Reg also feels that the older and more battered up a fly is, the better it fishes. When he tied bugs he wanted to make them perfect, but he noticed that it was often the rough-looking ones that hooked fish.

Reg believes that presentation is critical, but admits that even a bad cast will sometimes hook a fish.

Keith Piercey

Keith was born in St. John's in 1943. He moved to Corner Brook in 1962, where he now lives. Although he fished for trout and salmon while growing up on the Avalon Peninsula, it was when he moved to the West Coast of Newfoundland that his salmon fishing began in earnest. It was shortly after his move to Corner Brook that Keith began tying his own flies. A co-worker, Tom Cahill, was a fly tier and he taught Keith the basics. Keith also credits Veniards' *Fly Tying Guide* as being a big help when he was starting out. Later he attended Ron Alcott's workshop on tying classic salmon flies when he visited Corner Brook. Keith was very impressed with Ron Alcott's teaching.

The Peacock Flasher

Tag:	Surgeon's wire or other fine wire	Body:	Peacock herl
		Rib:	Two strands of blue Krystal Flash
Tail:	Golden pheasant with a small bit of pheasant tippet on top, about half the length	Throat:	Blue hackle
		Wing:	Fine black bear fur.
		Cheeks:	Jungle cock

Keith was also able to learn from the late Max Rabbitts. Max used to host an outdoors show on the local CBC station where Keith was working at the time, and Keith often talked to him about fishing and fly tying. Other local fly tiers who have been helpful to Keith include Paul Barnes and Paul Webb.

Keith tied commercially for a few years and sold his flies through a variety of outlets, including Ayres in Corner Brook. Although Keith no longer ties flies for sale, he continues to tie for himself and friends.

In Labrador he likes a pattern he calls the Pinware Purple. On the island, he prefers the dark flies like the Undertaker and the Blue Charm. For the latter's wing, he mostly uses red squirrel tail, though a lot of people use white calf tail.

Keith ties on a variety of hooks, such as Daiichi and Mustad, but is partial to Partridge Bartleet irons for his wet flies and uses Mustad 9672 hooks for his bombers and streamers. He also likes to use jungle cock eyes on his flies and believes that they add some extra allure to the fly. Keith has a unique and clever method of making the most of his jungle cock eyes: He splits the larger eyes into two or four strips, depending on the size, and uses the strips as eyes on his smaller flies. Now that he is retired from his job as a civil servant, Keith works several days a week in the Salmon Preservation Association for the Waters of Newfoundland office and he also serves as one of the assistant editors for *SPAWNER*.

Max Rabbitts

1912–1968

Max Rabbitts was a pioneer in the development of fly tying in Newfoundland and Labrador, and is perhaps one of the best-known early fly tiers in the province. Many of the tiers in western Newfoundland today were taught the basics of fly tying by Max Rabbitts.

Rabbitts was one of the founders of the Bay of Islands Rod and Gun Club, and served three terms as its president in the 1950s.

Ches Loughlin, one of his students, says that Max was an excellent fly tier who could tie the most complex traditional featherwing salmon patterns. "He was also a very innovative tier and he created simple but effective patterns using local materials," adds Ches. Rabbitts was well known in the Corner Brook area through his fly tying as well as his involvement in the Anglers Mart, a sporting goods store that he ran with Fred Clark. When John McDonald wrote his *Fortune* magazine

Guides Fly

Butt:	Yellow floss	Wing:	Brown calftail or
Body:	Black wool		squirrel tail

article on Atlantic salmon in 1948, he profiled fly tiers in eastern Canada who were developing new fly patterns for salmon. In Newfoundland he included two tiers, Ted Bugden and Max Rabbitts. The fly he included for Bugden was the Micmac Moose and for Rabbitts, the Guides pattern.

Although he is well known for his fly tying, perhaps the greatest contribution Max Rabbitts made to fly tying in Newfoundland and Labrador was as a teacher. In a profile featured in the 2004 issue of *SPAWNER* magazine, Don Hutchens wrote that Max taught his first fly-tying class in the fall of 1948 in his own home. He eventually began to teach at the Corner Brook Rod and Gun Club.

Several of the fly tiers in this book either attended classes taught by Max or received some help with some aspect of their fly tying from him. They remember him as a patient teacher who would work with them until they mastered whichever aspect of fly tying they were having difficulty with.

Max died on a fishing trip to Serpentine Lake in 1968, but his legacy lives on through his fly patterns as well as the innovative fly-tying styles and number of fly tiers now found in Newfoundland and Labrador.

Len Rich

Born in Whitehall, New York, in 1938, Len first came to Newfoundland when he was stationed at the Harmon Air Force Base in Stephenville. He left the service in 1964 and returned to the States for a two-year period before returning to Newfoundland, where he lived until 2004. He now lives in Nova Scotia.

Len began tying flies in 1966, in Stephenville. His fly-tying neighbour, Ignatius Hall, got him started, and Paul Barnes later gave him some pointers.

Len set up a cardex system to catalogue every trout and salmon pattern he could find, and used it as a reference to help his tying.

He was tying what he calls the standard salmon patterns: the Thunder and Lightning and Blue Charm, as well as local patterns such as the Silver Tip. He was also constantly experimenting with different patterns and tying styles: "If I was tying a dry fly pattern I would also tie one up as a wet fly, or if I was tying a wet I would also tie up some in a dry fly style. That way if I rose a salmon with either a wet or dry, I knew they were interested in something about that particular fly, so I could offer it to them as a dry or wet." Len says his approach worked at least enough times to keep him tying that way.

Big Intervale Blue

Tag:	Oval gold tinsel	Rib:	Oval gold tinsel
Tail:	Golden pheasant crest	Wing:	White polar bear hair or
Body:	Brilliant Royal Blue floss,		substitute
	tied full	Collar:	Silver Doctor blue hackle

Living in western Newfoundland provided Len with many opportunities to fish for both trout and salmon, and he took advantage of them, fishing every weekend during the salmon season.

Len's favourite wet fly for Atlantic salmon is the Blue Charm, which he feels works well everywhere, but he says his own Big Intervale Blue—which many anglers in this book favour—is a close second. "That pattern has been very good to me," he says. "Blue has always been a popular colour—look at the Blue Charm— but I believe the key to this fly is the polar bear hair. It has a translucency that shows up very well in the water."

Len favours Wilson low-water hooks for his salmon flies, preferring the light wire for both wet and dry flies. He also uses Mustad bronze down eye hooks for some of his flies.

Len believes the most important aspects of a fly are colour and size. He likes a fairly full-bodied fly and will often double-wrap the body to build up some bulk.

Len worked for the Newfoundland and Labrador government for several years to promote and develop hunting and fishing in the province. When he retired from government, he began to develop the Awesome Lake Lodge in Labrador. The lodge opened in 1990, and Len ran it for ten years before selling it to its current owners. He continues to be involved in the business, and helps to promote and market the lodge at outdoor sport shows during the winter, as well as traveling to the lodge every summer to help manage it.

Len is familiar to many anglers and fly tiers through his writing. When he lived in Corner Brook, he wrote a weekly outdoor column for the *Western Star* and also served as the founding editor for *SPAWNER* magazine from 1979 to 1985. His first book, *Newfoundland Salmon Flies and How to Tie Them*, was released in 1985 and was the first book to profile flies from Atlantic Canada. His other books include *Best of In The Woods* (1990), *Fly Fishing Tips and Tactics* (1999), *River and Woods* (2002), *Tales of Christmas* (2003), and *So You Want to be An Outfitter* (2005).

Earl Roberts

From his innovative use of markers to colour his flies to his willingness to try different patterns, Earl Roberts epitomizes the innovative fly-tying style of many East Coast fly tiers. Born in Twillingate in 1951, Earl moved with his parents to Corner Brook when he was thirteen. He grew up there and eventually became a physical edu-

Lime Cosseboom

Tag:	Oval silver	Rib:	Oval silver
Tip:	Fluorescent red floss	Wing:	Black squirrel
Butt:	Ostrich herl	Hackle:	Lime green collared
Body:	Lime green floss	Head:	Black

cation instructor at C. C. Loughlin School. He was introduced to salmon fishing in 1970.

In 1975 Earl bought a fly-tying kit, which contained a vice and a few tools, and started taking flies apart to see how they had been constructed. Later he took a fly-tying course offered at a local school. He enjoyed fly tying so much that he eventually became a fly-tying instructor himself and taught for many years.

At one time, Earl tied flies commercially for Dennis Drover, who operated a Sports Experts store in Corner Brook, but these days he ties for his own use and to give to friends. "Newfoundland must be the hardest place in the world for a commercial fly tier to make a living," Earl told me. "Almost everyone ties their own flies or has someone in the family who ties."

Like many western Newfoundland fly tiers, Earl remembers meeting Max Rabbitts, and says Max introduced him to fly tying in that part of Newfoundland.

Earl is a big fan of the Cosseboom fly, especially tied on a streamer hook. He likes to ties it on a Mustad 79580 hook, and sometimes open up the gape a bit with a pair of pliers.

To show the fish something different, Earl uses flies that have a different shape than the norm. One of these is the Upside-Down fly, developed by late Corner Brook tier Rocky Schulstad.

Earl colours his fly-tying materials, and his approach to this is fairly innovative: he uses onion skins as a dye, and uses markers to change the colour of hackle or bodies. He even brings the markers with him to the river, so he can quickly change the colours of his flies. He also likes to enhance the colour of the butts and bodies of his flies. He does this either by adding a layer of silver tinsel to the hook shank before tying the fly or by painting the hook shanks with white enamel paint. He often ties his flies with fluorescent bodies and butts, and his lime green Cosseboom was featured in Len Rich's *Newfoundland Salmon Flies and How to Tie Them.*

Earl only uses moosehair for the wings of the Upside-Down fly or the Blue Charm; for most of his salmon flies he prefers squirrel tail, finding that it doesn't flare as much as the moose hair does.

Earl is a strong supporter of catch-and-release angling for salmon and feels that the fishing in the last three years has improved greatly compared to that of the 1980s and '90s. However, he is still concerned about poaching on some of the West Coast rivers, and the number of inshore nets set for herring and mackerel worries him. "Those nets are set along the shore and they can't help but catch salmon," says Earl.

Martin "Rocky" Schulstad

Rocky Schulstad was born in British Columbia and first came to Newfoundland during World War Two. He met his future wife, Georgina, in St. John's, and after the war they returned to British Columbia. However, the pull of Newfoundland was hard to resist and in 1948 they returned to St. John's, where Rocky found work as a journalist and photographer for the *Evening Telegram*. Eventually they settled in Corner Brook, where Rocky worked with Bowater's Newfoundland Pulp and Paper company as their press officer. During his time at Bowater, Rocky would provide guiding services to the company's business clients who visited Newfoundland. Much of his guiding took place on the Serpentine River, where Bowater had a fishing lodge.

Rocky was well known as an angler, photographer and fly tier. Some of the fly patterns he created include classic Newfoundland fly patterns such as the Silver Tip, Texas Jim Stonefly, Charbell and Papoose. He was a creative fly tier, as evidenced by his development of the Upside-Down moosehair fly, designed to show fish something different.

Rocky's Texas Jim Stonefly was featured as one of the "Deadly Dozen" salmon flies in the first issue of *SPAWNER* in 1979. Rocky's write-up outlined how the fly was developed around 1965 while he was guiding two anglers on the Serpentine River. One of the anglers was a newspaper man from Texas named Jim Barnett. Rocky had tied the fly to imitate a small yellow stonefly that was common on the river, and when Jim Barnett made his first cast with the fly, he caught his first Atlantic salmon. The fly would account for forty-seven fish during the remainder of that week and it secured a place for itself in Newfoundland fly-tying history.

With his background in journalism, Rocky was instrumental in producing the first edition of *SPAWNER*. Ches Loughlin, current *SPAWNER* editor, says that Rocky was a great help: "He showed us how to lay out the magazine and even provided the picture for the cover." Rocky passed away in 1998 and his contribution to sport fishing in Newfoundland and Labrador was recognized when he was inducted to SPAWN's Hall of Fame.

Rocky's Texas Jim Stonefly is still a good fly for big fish on the Lower Humber, and his Silvertip remains a great fly both on Newfoundland and in Labrador.

Rocky's Upside-Down Moosehair Fly

Tag: Oval silver
Tail: Golden pheasant crest
Body: Black wool

Wing: Black hackle
Throat: Moose hair

John Sheppard

John was born in 1946 in Pools Island, Bonavista Bay, but grew up in Cormack along the banks of the Humber River. Today he lives in Gander, where he works as coordinator of the skills upgrading program for the College of the North Atlantic, and returns to Cormack every summer.

John began fly tying in 1963 when an uncle gave him a fly-tying kit with Thompson tools and materials from Veniards. His first efforts (a couple of Blue Charms) were not too successful, but after a year's hiatus he tried again and stuck with it.

John gave his first flies away to anglers in the community; as his flies caught fish, demand grew and he began to sell them. His father grew tired of people coming to the house at all hours looking for the flies, and in 1975 opened Sheppard's Store in Cormack, which John continues to operate in the summer. John has another business, Straight Line Sports, in Gander, which he runs the rest of the year. He runs a very busy fly-tying and wholesaling business, with over twenty tiers supplying him with flies. Most years he sells between 200,000 and 250,000 flies, ranging from trout and salmon flies to saltwater rigs for cod and mackerel. John also runs a custom rod-building business using Loomis blanks.

John cites Edson Leonard's *Flies* as being useful early on in his fly tying (he has thirty years' worth of fly-fishing and fly-tying magazines, too). He attended workshops hosted by Ron Alcott and Charles Krom, and eventually developed his own style and began to be in demand as a teacher himself. He taught several classes in Gander and hosted a series of fly-tying and rod-building shows on the Gander cable network.

John's favourite salmon fly is "The Silver Cosseboom, no question," he says, adding that he ties his flies small, sizes 10 to 12, including his bombers, for which he usually uses a #10 Mustad 9672. He ties his bugs and bombers with natural

"Selecting one of Farlow's lovely 'silver doctors,' I commenced at the head of the upper pool, whilst Jim fished below. About one-third down, a rise! And I was fast in a 3 lb. trout, which was speedily landed, and to cut a long story short, I took out of that pool before I left it eighteen others, averaging from 2 lb. to 3 lb. I then moved down to help Jim, who could not get his line out to the further bank where the fish lay; so together we went down to the rattle and pool below. At this place we found the trout 'jostling each other,' so thick were they that, although there were salmon in the pool (we could see them), they stood no chance, as the more nimble trout seized the fly immediately it touched the water."

W. R. Kennedy,
Sport Travel and Adventure in Newfoundland and the West Indies
(1881)

Little Codroy River Fly

Thread:	White uni-thread 8/0	Wing:	Grey squirrel tail
Body:	Silver Mylar tinsel size 12	Head:	Red
Throat:	Hackle, yellow schlappen		

caribou hair, but if a pattern calls for a different colour he uses deerhair; he finds it takes the dye better than caribou.

John likes a well-proportioned, durable fly, but doesn't have much preference in terms of colour or pattern—he leaves that up to the angler. He doesn't mind changing the colour of a butt or wing to provide something different and he is not averse to making changes when he is on the water. "I don't mind barberizing them if I want a sparser pattern," he says. "I want to do justice to the art and provide good quality flies."

His best sellers are, in order, the Silver Blue, the Silver Cosseboom, and the Blue Charm tied with either a moose or calftail wing. John is not surprised the Blue Charm or Thunder and Lightning, tied with white wings, have been very popular in Newfoundland shops recently. "I like calf body hair but it's hard to find it long enough for larger flies, so I often use calftail for size 6 and up," he says.

John ties on a Thompson vice, and is a big fan of their fly-tying tools. He uses 6/0 or 8/0 uni-thread and doesn't use a whipping tool to finish his flies: "I prefer to use my hands, and I sometimes tie without using a vice if I'm using a bigger hook."

John has developed a large number of different patterns and series of flies. A partial list includes the Humber, Gold and Silver, Cormack and Dark Water Series, as well as the Polar Baits, flies he developed for ice fishing. He created a series of 177 salmon flies, one for each of the 177 Atlantic salmon rivers in Newfoundland and Labrador, and is still developing new patterns. His latest efforts include a series of soft hackle flies as well as a group he calls Hot Heads, so named because they all have coloured heads—fluorescent orange, yellow, chartreuse, green, and so on. He ties them on a Mustad 3906 hook.

John's series of flies for the Codroy River were featured in the 2003 issue of *SPAWNER* magazine.

Rob Solo

Rob was born in Grand Falls in 1958 and moved with his family to Corner Brook in 1964. Rob works as a goldsmith but arranges his work schedule so he has most summers off to guide salmon fishers. He has a photographic memory when it comes to fishing and fly tying. He remembers catching his first trout, a four-and-a-half-pound sea trout, on a #10 Silver Doctor. Rob began salmon fishing in 1972 when he was seventeen, but it took him three years before he caught his first

Hair Hackle Black Cosseboom

Tag:	Oval silver tinsel and fluorescent orange nylon	Hackle:	Yellow deerhair spun on as a collar
Body:	Black chenille or wool	Head:	Red
Wing:	Dark brown squirrel tail		

fish. He says it was on the South West River, July 8, 1975, at 9:45 PM, on a #6 moose-hair Green Highlander.

Rob began fly tying in 1972, first on his own, then under the instruction of Merle Yarn. Thus began a serious study of fly fishing and fly tying that continues to this day. On the advice of his uncle, Rob began to carefully watch how other salmon anglers fished, and to ask a lot of questions. He sought out professionals, too, first writing to Lee Wulff at the age of fourteen. Wulff replied, establishing a long-lived correspondence. Rob went down to Wulff's home and attended the fly-fishing school that Wulff and his wife Joan conducted. He also took courses from Ron Alcott in tying classic salmon flies. He began tying commercially in the 1980s—he once tied twelve hundred flies in one month to fill an order—but has since stopped. "It was a lot of work for very little return," he laughs.

Rob credits four books as being instrumental in his fly tying: Wulff's *The Atlantic Salmon,* Terri Hellekson's *Popular Fly Patterns*, Art Flick's *Master Fly Tying Guide* and John Veniard's *Fly Tying Problems and Their Answers.*

Rob ties some traditional salmon flies, and a featherwing Green Highlander helped him catch his first big salmon on the Humber River. "I love the history surrounding the old patterns as well as the material used to tie them," he says. However, the material is difficult to obtain these days, and recently Rob began experimenting with another material, synthetic living fibre (SLF), which mimics the natural materials. He has also tested the Enrico Puglisi (EP) fibre, which he obtained from a manufacturer in New York.

Rob pioneered the use of deerhair for hackle in 1985 and believes its effectiveness is due in part to the fact that a fly tied with deerhair rides higher in the water. Also, deer hair doesn't darken like hackle often does, so it remains bright even in the evening.

Rob favours Daichi hooks for his wet flies but switches to the Aled Jackson Spey flies for his bigger flies.

The Orange Riffle, which Rob developed in 1978, is his favourite fly, especially for the Lower Humber. In it, he combined the body and hackle of a Thunder and Lightning with the wing and style of Lee Wulff's Lady Joan fly. He thought that, since he fished the fly hitched and it would be moving fairly quickly in the water, tying on a tag, tail and butts wasn't necessary.

Rob has converted many trout flies to salmon patterns and is constantly experimenting with new patterns and techniques. He believes that neatness, correct proportions, and durability make the best fly. Key to durability are, he says, "the best material combined with correct tying procedure and the right cement." Rob uses cement such as Dave's Flexament throughout the tying process, but he always finishes his flies with a coat of celluire from Veniards or Anglers Corner head cement—never nail polish: "That stuff always turns milky," he laughs.

Although Rob wants his flies to look right, he also believes presentation is critical: "Anglers have to be aware of environmental conditions when they fish," he says. When the air is colder, "the fish may not be surface-minded, so you should plan on going deeper."

Rob Solo's PEI fly was featured in the series of fishing stamps released in 2005.

Rob favours the evening as the best time to salmon fish, and he has an interesting theory on what attracts Newfoundland salmon to a fly: "Most Newfoundland streams aren't fertile and the insect hatches are not that rich, so nymphs are not available. As a result, young salmon parr depend more on terrestrial insects as a food source. So the salmon are more surface-minded than they are in other areas." Rob credits this preference for the effectiveness of the Portland Creek or Riffling hitch, and believes that the farther north you go in Newfoundland, the more important the fly becomes.

Rob's flies have appeared in several fly-tying books, including Stewart and Allen's *Flies for Atlantic Salmon* as well as Paul Marriner's *Modern Atlantic Salmon Flies*. He is an active outdoors writer whose fishing and fly-tying articles have appeared in several publications. He is presently putting the final touches on a book entitled *Dressing Durable and Effective Atlantic Salmon Flies,* which he hopes to publish shortly.

Bas Vokey

Bas was born in St. John's in 1922 and has lived there all his life. For many years he worked with Trans-Canada Airlines, which later became Air Canada. Although he fished all his life, Bas didn't begin fly tying until 1960, when he purchased a fly-tying kit from Veniards as a Christmas gift for one of his sons. He began tying flies with his son and was soon hooked. His first ties were classic English patterns with married featherwings, but he gradually switched over to moosehair wings.

Over time Bas developed his own tying style and began teaching, offering evening courses through the recreation department in St. John's as well as an extension course in fly tying for Memorial University.

Bas always enjoyed teaching: "One of my greatest pleasures is looking back at some of my students and being able to say, 'the students have surpassed the teacher,'" he says. Bas taught fly tying for over twenty years and estimates he has taught over four hundred fly tiers in his lifetime.

Bas first tied commercially for Howie Meeker, the former NHL player. Meeker hosted a local television show and asked Bas to come on and talk about fly tying and fishing. After the show, Meeker asked Bas to tie some flies for the Meeker Sport Shop in St. John's. This was the beginning of a prolific career—Bas esti-

Polar White

Tail:	Badger hackle	Hackle:	Light badger
Body:	Beige floss	Wing:	Polar bear

mates that while he tied commercially, he averaged six thousand flies a year, tying two to three hundred of one pattern at a time, all while working full time and raising a family.

In addition to Meeker's Shop, he also tied for Harrison Hiscock and the Sport Shop. Other orders came from commercial salmon camps in central Newfoundland. One of Bas's sons lived in Gander, and through him Bas was able to supply many of the salmon fishing camps on the Gander. Some orders came from unlikely places: "One year my son and I received an order for salmon flies from Indian Beer, a popular Newfoundland brewing company. As a promotion, if you purchased a half dozen beer you received a fly. We tied five thousand for that one promotion, mostly Silvertips, Blue Charms and other moosehair patterns."

Through his work in the public relations department with the airline, Bas was often asked to host visiting VIPs who wanted to fish while in Newfoundland. One of the anglers Bas tied flies for was the editor of *The Field*, a well-known British sporting magazine. Bas says the editor was impressed with his simple moosehair flies, which he described as flies "without the damn fur and feathers."

The airline work has also given Bas the opportunity to fish for tuna with A. J. Mclane and for salmon with Lee Wulff, on River of Ponds. His time with Wulff led to the creation of one of his patterns, the Polar White: "I watched Wulff fish his White Wulff fly and later attempted to duplicate the fly. I didn't have any kip [calftail], so I substituted polar bear hair instead." The hair laid flat, unlike calftail, but the flies were successful nonetheless.

Bas purchased many of his materials in bulk from Herters, later repackaging and selling some of them to his fly-tying students. He also purchased materials from Veniards and Hardy in England, and used primarily Mustad hooks.

Bas believes there is no money in fly tying today, and that most Newfoundland and Labrador salmon anglers tie their own flies or have friends who supply them.

Bas's fly-tying video has sold about one thousand copies, and he owns the copyright to the Newfoundland Fly, which he developed and sells at tourism outlets throughout the province.

Frank Walsh

Frank was born in 1951 in St. John's, where he works as an accountant with the provincial government. He fished for trout as a young boy and was sixteen when his friend Charlie Kendall taught him how to tie. Frank began salmon fishing a year later during a trip to Indian Bay River, but it would take him five or six

Stimulator

Tail:	Elk hair	Thorax:	Amber Antron
Body:	Yellow Antron	Thorax:	Grizzly
Body:	Furnace	Head:	Red
Wing:	Elk hair		

rivers before he landed his first fish, a grilse, from Travers Brook near Gambo.

Frank ties a few flies commercially and for custom orders. He and Ian Gall tie flies—some years up to thirty or forty dozen—for donations to the Salmon Protection Association for the Waters of Newfoundland and the Salmon Association of Eastern Newfoundland.

Frank has a great interest in tying traditional featherwing Atlantic salmon flies, and has attended Ron Alcott's fly-tying workshops on tying classic salmon flies, which he finds quite a challenge.

Frank ties some of the neatest, most meticulous flies around, but claims there's no secret to his tying: "I tie all my flies using white thread so the colour doesn't bleed through, and I use good materials," he says.

His favourite wet fly for salmon is the hair hackle Black Cosseboom. Rob Solo developed the technique of using deerhair as hackle, and Frank thinks it makes a great fly. The Orange Bug with a split wing is his favourite dry fly.

For trout, Frank likes Wulffs, and lately he has been tying the Stimulator. He ties on an HMH rotary, which he is happy with.

Frank ties up to a hundred dozen trout and salmon flies a year, and the pastime continues to give him a great deal of pleasure.

Paul Webb

Although his name may not be familiar to many, Paul's flies are recognizable. His traditional featherwing salmon fly called the Humber September appeared on the cover of the 2004 issue of *SPAWNER*.

Born in 1969 in Corner Brook, Paul still lives there. He began fly fishing when he was eight or nine and fly tying when he was ten, when he received a tying kit for Christmas. He used the included instructional manual, and also watched his grandfather tie flies. His grandfather also had a fly-tying book from Veniards, *A Fly Dresser's Guide*, which was very helpful to Paul when he was starting out.

Paul soon mastered most fly-tying patterns and became interested in tying featherwing salmon flies—first the simpler ones and soon more difficult patterns. One of his flies won the Global Fly Fisher Award in 2001.

Paul is not content with simply tying or fishing standard patterns, and he is constantly developing and fishing new trout and salmon flies. One of his favourite flies for trout is a dragonfly nymph he developed. For salmon, he likes a hairwing

Calftail Blue Charm

Tip:	Fine oval silver tinsel	Throat:	Dyed blue calftail (medium to dark blue)
Tag:	Chartreuse floss		
Tail:	Golden pheasant crest	Wing:	Fine black moose
Body:	Black floss	Head:	Black
Ribs:	Oval silver tinsel		

Blue Charm with a fluorescent butt. He prefers a fairly full fly, and often uses new material such as synthetic living fibre (SLF) as wing material in traditional salmon flies like the Jock Scott and Green Highlander. While he uses Mustad bronze down eye hooks for most of his trout flies, he favours Tiemco hooks for his salmon flies: "They are a nice hook, very sharp and with a small barb," he says.

Lee Wulff

1905–1991

When Lee Wulff died in a crash of his light plane in 1991, the angling world lost one of its giants. Many consider him to be the most influential angler of the twentieth century and few have contributed as much to our knowledge of fishing for trout and salmon. His legacy lives on in the flies he developed, his books and videos, and the fishing equipment he invented. As an author and teacher, Lee was a leading voice for the conservation of trout and salmon. As early as 1939 he recognized the effect that over-fishing was having on salmon and he coined the phrase, "A good game fish is too valuable to be caught only once."

Although he was an American, Lee was no stranger to Atlantic Canada. He often came here to fish and his first experiences as a salmon fisherman were gained on the Margaree, Ecum Secum and St. Mary's rivers in Nova Scotia. In a letter he wrote to the Margaree Salmon Museum, now on display there, he wrote, "The Margaree was my first love among salmon rivers."

While he also fished in New Brunswick, it was in Newfoundland and Labrador that he left his greatest mark. Through his work for the tourism department he did a great deal of work on popularizing sport fishing and hunting. Later, through his lodges, he introduced many anglers to the joy of fishing for Atlantic salmon and brook trout on the rivers and lakes of both Newfoundland and Labrador.

Wulff was also a prolific author, and his book *The Atlantic Salmon* is a standard reference on the sport of fly fishing for this species.

In addition to his books and videos, Lee invented the modern fly-fishing vest and the triangle taper fly line. He was also a well-known fly tier and designer. Seldom using a vice, he was able to tie the smallest fly while holding the hook in his fingers.

Best known as a salmon angler, he also did a great deal of trout fishing. His greatest contribution to angling was arguably his series of Wulff flies, originally designed for trout but remarkably effective on almost any fish. The Wulff series—the Royal, White, Black and AuSable, as well as the many variations that now exist—are found in most anglers' fly boxes. Although he is no longer with us, Lee's legacy of fishing knowledge, his flies and his conservation ethic will live on.

Chapter

Fly Tiers
of Nova Scotia

"But for solid comfort, pure and simple, with a modicum of fun, recommend me to the rivers and hospitality of Nova Scotia. In the first place, the fishing is not bad, while there is the omnipresent compensation of civilization always within reach."

Charles Hallock,
The Salmon Fisher *(1890)*

From the highlands of Cape Breton to the misty lakes of Yarmouth County, Nova Scotia has something to offer every angler. There are thirty-seven species in the province; four of them (rainbow trout, brown trout, small-mouth bass and chain pickerel) are the result of human intervention in the last hundred years.

Each season brings its own fishing opportunities. In the spring anglers search for the first blue of open water as they wait for ice to leave inland lakes—which sometimes doesn't happen until mid-May in northern Nova Scotia and Cape Breton, though the rest of the province allows earlier access to lakes and streams. Many anglers brave snow, rain and cold for Fishing Opening Day in April. Brook trout is the traditional quarry for these early-season fishers. The most popular sport-fish in the province, it is also the most widespread, found in almost all watersheds.

May brings softer winds, warmer temperatures and the mayfly. Fishing the yearly mayfly hatch is a time-honoured tradition for many Nova Scotia anglers.

The first rise of water in July used to signal the arrival of Atlantic salmon runs to the province's rivers; however, in recent years, global warming, combined with acid rain and poor ocean survival, has severely reduced many salmon runs to a shadow of their former glory. Fortunately some exceptions exist, as in the case of Cape Breton's Margaree River as well as the rivers running into the Northumberland Strait in northern Nova Scotia. These rivers still meet spawning escapement requirements and provide excellent angling opportunities in the fall.

Joe Aucoin

In 1935 Joseph Louis Barrow, better known to boxing fans as Joe Louis, was making a name for himself among the ranks of heavyweight contenders. During this period he was given the nickname "The Brown Bomber" for his exploits in the ring. While his prowess as a prizefighter was earning him recognition all around the world, he would receive special recognition from an unlikely corner. In the coal-mining town of New Waterford on Cape Breton Island, Nova Scotia, a local fly tier, Joe Aucoin, would craft a fly in honour of the fighter.

Joe worked as a miner in New Waterford's #12 Colliery. An accident in the mine severely injured his back, and although he continued working for the twenty remaining years of his life, he lived in constant pain. Like other fly tiers in Eastern Canada during the 1930s and '40s, Joe was a pioneer in the development of hairwing Atlantic salmon flies, which would later prove to be a major influence on the sport. From his home in New Waterford, he sold flies and leaders and did some guiding during the annual miners' vacation in the summer.

Edson Leonard's classic book *Flies*, first published in 1950, contains a letter Joe wrote to Leonard in 1949. It provides patterns for Joe's bomber series, Ross Special, Yellow Bucktail and Mystery, revealing that the Silver Gray Bomber "saved the day and fishing trip many a time."

Joe's letter also states that his patterns were fished in Scotland during the war and had often out-fished older, traditional patterns. Joe thought his flies were successful because they were more lifelike; in his words, "they have a breathing action in the water." This action was due to the long wings he used in his patterns, often twice as long as the shank of the hook.

Many beginning fly tiers have been told not to extend wings beyond the hook bend in order to avoid the "short takers," but the effectiveness of his flies suggests that Aucoin was onto something. No less an authority than Joseph Bates gives this piece of advice to tiers in *The Art of the Atlantic Salmon Fly*: "Don't be concerned about the long wing and salmon striking short. If they want the fly they will have it!"

Another striking characteristic of Joe Aucoin's flies was the size of jungle cock he use—in his flies, the eye often extended the full length of the body.

Rick MacDonald from Sydney, Cape Breton, widely known and respected as the dean of Cape Breton fly tiers, fished with Joe and is able to shed some light on the length of his flies. Rick suggests that as a commercial fly tier, Joe used all the regular-

Brown Bomber

Tail:	Golden pheasant crest	Rib:	Oval silver
Tag:	Silver tinsel	Hackle:	Brown
Tip:	Yellow floss	Wing:	Fox squirrel tail
Butt:	Black chenille	Cheeks:	Jungle cock eye
Body:	Brown wool	Topping:	Golden pheasant crest

sized jungle cock on the flies he was selling. This left him with only very small or large eyes for his own personal flies. When he found the patterns tied with the large eyes out-fished the others, he began using them in his commercial business.

Jack Aucoin and Annette Bates, Joe's son and daughter, both say that fly tying was an important part of their lives when they were growing up: "Dad dyed his own material so I remember that there was always some deerhair drying behind the stove," Annette says. "He also did up leaders to sell and he would dye them in a coffee can that was put on the back of the coal stove in the kitchen."

Annette and Jack also helped their father with his flies. "I was the quality control," laughs Annette. "I looked at each one after he tied it, put the head cement on, and after it dried, packaged them up. Jack would take them up to the post office on his bicycle."

Joe made very little money from fly tying. "He used to tie for the Sports Shop in Sydney and instead of getting paid, he would take sporting goods for the boys. When we spent the summer in Margaree he would be selling flies at stores operated by Bernie Doyle and Jim Smith. Instead of taking money for the flies they sold, he would get groceries or tobacco," says Annette.

Both Annette and Jack remember their father being fussy about the materials he used for his flies, especially his hooks. He ordered a lot of material from Veniards—enough that the company sent Joe's wife a sympathy card when Joe passed away.

Annette says that her father tied every day and there was a Black Bomber in his vice when he died. She also told me that her father would use a variety of materials when tying his flies. "Dad had a dog, a collie named Prancer. He loved that dog, and sometimes he would snip some hair off him to tie up a fly."

Edson Leonard's *Flies* introduced Aucoin's hairwing salmon flies to the world. Later they were also featured in A. J. McClane's *Standard Fishing Encyclopedia*, Joe Bates's *Atlantic Salmon Flies and Fishing*, Dr. Grey's *Handbook for the Margaree* and, more recently, in Stewart and Allen's *Flies for Atlantic Salmon*. The 1948 *Fortune* article "Atlantic Salmon" featured the bomber series as well as the Ross Special, which Joe tied for his friend Nip Ross.

Joe passed away in 1968, and unfortunately, many of the patterns he developed or helped to popularize have fallen out of use, with the exception of the Ross Special, which continues to be a popular fall pattern in Nova Scotia. But Joe's Black, Brown and Silver Gray Bombers have played an important role in the development of our sport and deserve our respect. Besides, you never know when they may save the day!

Reg Baird

Reg was born in 1935 in Clementsvale, Nova Scotia. After high school, he went to work for his father, Donald Baird, in his general store. Reg took over the business in 1976 and ran it until he retired in 1999. Reg is known by anglers in Atlantic Canada

Invincible Ghost

Tail:	Mallard flank barbules		saddle hackle under one
Body:	Rear half silver tinsel,		badger saddle hackle on
	front half black floss or		each side
	black dubbing fur	Shoulder:	Mallard flank feather
Rib:	Fine gold tinsel		tied one-third length of
Wing:	White marabou or white		body
	goat hair with one blue	Cheek:	Jungle cock

through his Snow Country business, which sold trapping and fishing equipment for many years.

Reg began fly fishing at an early age with his father. "I caught my first trout when I was five years old and fell out of a canoe when I was six years old," laughs Reg. Reg's father tied flies and Reg soon picked it up. "We always fished with a dropper fly, even if we were fishing with bait."

Reg began tying flies in earnest in 1959 following a salmon fishing trip to New-foundland. His guide, Edgar Eastman, gave him simple but effective moosehair patterns. When he got home, Reg started tying his own flies. A neighbour, George Kregling, taught Reg the basics.

Reg soon was tying flies to match the insect hatches on his home waters. He credits Swisher and Richard's book *Fly Fishing Strategies* for helping him with his study of what trout were eating and how to imitate their food. He purchased some fly-tying material from Eric Leiser in the United States and the two soon began corresponding. They exchanged flies, and two of Reg's patterns—the Little Stonefly and Reg's Hellgrammite—appear in Leiser's book. Reg sometimes varies the Hellgrammite pattern by using a lacquered peacock herl head and a brown emu feather tied on top of the hook.

Reg tied commercially for twenty-five years when he ran the store and he con-tinues to tie for custom orders, for donations to conservation groups, and for him-self. He likes his flies sparse and believes how a fly moves in or on the water is critical to its success.

When he tied commercially, Reg had to tie by the book, but now he likes to experiment with different materials. One substitution Reg has found successful is using marabou for streamer wings instead of hair: "I wet the marabou before I tie it in so I will get the correct amount in the wing. I used to wet the feathers in my mouth but started wondering what the chemicals in the dye might be doing to me, so now I keep a bowl of water by the vice and wet the feathers with my fingers. Un-less you see what the fly will look like when it is wet, it is hard to get the amount right; it will either be too bulky or too sparse."

When he was in business, Reg dyed much of his fly-tying material, finding that it was the only way he could match the colours of local hatches. He often used a photo-dyeing technique developed by Harry Darbee. "We used to use Indian game cock necks and dye them with silver nitrate, which was used for developing black-and-white film. If you took a cream-coloured neck and dyed it with this technique, it came out with a beautiful bronze dun that had a sparkle about it that was very effective." The technique waned as the availability of genetic hackle from Metz eliminated the need to dye hackle for many patterns.

Reg feels that presentation is an important part of successful trout fly fishing. "While you want to match what the fish are eating as closely as possible, I also believe that the wrong fly fished right will out-fish the right fly fished wrong."

Reg has developed several successful patterns. One of his favourites is a streamer, the Invincible Ghost: "A friend, the late Bernie Baxter, used to fish for brown trout with a streamer he called the Invincible Minnow," recalls Reg. "While Bernie was alive I didn't want to betray a trust, so I never told anyone about the pattern. I modified it by using white marabou wings and since I am a big fan of the Black Ghost, I called it the Invincible Ghost." Another of Reg's patterns, the Orange Caddis, came about as he attempted to imitate an orange caddis that came off the water during the evening hatch in Kejimkujik National Park.

Reg has been the angling editor at *Eastern Woods and Waters* magazine since its inception in 1985 and has written extensively on fly fishing and fly tying. He has also published two books on trapping techniques. Reg is presently working on a book entitled *The Flies and Techniques of a Mersey River Guide*, which is due to be published shortly. He is active in sport-fish conservation in Nova Scotia and serves on the board of directors of Trout Nova Scotia.

Donnie Barnes

Donnie was born in Sherbrooke in 1938. The son of well-known Nova Scotia fly tier Henry Barnes, Donnie was exposed to fishing and fly tying at an early age. The family home, above Sherbrooke jail, was a favourite local gathering spot. "Several times a week the old-timers would gather at our place and the talk always turned to hunting, fishing and fly tying."

Donnie caught his first salmon, a grilse, in the St. Mary's River when he was eight years old, and he began tying flies when he was fifteen. After finishing school in 1955, he joined the Royal Canadian Air Force, where he served as an aircraft maintenance technician for twenty-six years. On retirement, he and his family returned to Sherbrooke, and he began working with the Department of Fisheries and Oceans as a conservation officer, a career he continued until he retired a second time in 1997.

Donnie learned how to tie flies from his father, and favours the simple patterns developed for the St. Mary's River. He prefers a sparse fly but varies his tying to meet water conditions. For some of his fall flies, he uses Mustad 36890 hooks as big as 3/0. He uses the Yellow Bucktail for much of his fishing, especially in the fall, and finds it works particularly well on the Margaree. During the summer, he uses a simple squirrel tail pattern his father developed for fishing grilse, and finds it successful in Nova Scotia and Newfoundland.

During his time in the air force, Donnie experienced some great salmon fishing around the country: "The military used to have a fishing camp on the Eagle River in Labrador and we had to be there to maintain the aircraft they were using to

Squirrel Tail Fly

Thread:	Black	Hackle:	Grizzly throat
Tail:	Golden pheasant crest	Wing:	Red squirrel tail
Rib:	Fine oval silver	Head:	Black
Body:	Black wool		

fly people in. During down time we were able to fish. I had twelve trips in there while I was in the service and we had fantastic fishing." Donnie was also based in Gander, Newfoundland, for part of his military career so he took advantage of the opportunity to fish the Gander, Exploits, Conne, Humber and other Newfoundland rivers.

He found that the flies he used on the St. Mary's worked just as well in Newfoundland and Labrador. A Cosseboom tied with a black body rather than the traditional green was particularly effective.

Donnie is also an avid trout angler and likes to use the MacIntosh fly, tied in smaller sizes such as #10 and #12, for most of his trout fishing. He guides during the season but says that, with the decline in salmon runs on the St. Mary's, business is slow these days. He continues to tie flies for family and friends and will do custom orders, but doesn't consider himself a commercial tier. "I used to tie flies for the late Jack Anderson at his store but eventually gave it up. Jack wanted the flies to be big, bulky and fully dressed so the fishermen would buy them, but I didn't like tying them that way so I gave it up."

Henry Barnes

1912–1968

Henry was born in St. Margaret's Bay, Nova Scotia. When he was fourteen years old his mother died, and Henry and his brother moved to Sherbrooke to work in the woods for the C. W. Anderson Lumber Company. Later he worked in gold mines throughout Nova Scotia, from Goldenville and Walton to Italy Cross. Henry eventually returned to Sherbrooke in 1945 to work as a meat cutter at Anderson's store and served as the town jailer. He and his family lived above the jail and that is where he did much of his fly tying. Henry's son Donnie, profiled above, told me that his father was the last jailer in Sherbrooke; when he passed away, the jail was closed and the prisoners transferred to Antigonish.

Donnie believes that his father picked up fly tying on his own from watching other tiers in the Sherbrooke area. Henry tied flies to sell at Anderson's store as well as on the river, and he always had a box of flies in his back pocket in case people wanted to buy one or two. Most of the time, he sold them for fifty cents.

Fly-tying material was hard to come by at that time, so Henry had to scrounge whatever was available to craft his flies. Donnie remembers his father scraping the paint off empty toothpaste tubes and then cutting them into narrow strips to use

Yellow Bucktail

Thread:	Black	Hackle:	Yellow saddle or neck, two turns
Tail:	Golden pheasant crest		
Body:	Black wool	Cheeks:	Jungle cock
Wing:	Yellow bucktail, sparse	Head:	Black

as tinsel on his flies. Henry used squirrel and deer tails as wing material, along with wool for bodies and feathers from Rhode Island Red chickens for hackle. He had a friend in Detroit, Ralph Campbell, who came home to fish the St. Mary's every year, and kept Henry supplied with material like jungle cock. Henry also ordered from Herters. He usually tied about a dozen flies every evening.

In the spring and in high water, Henry usually fished the Yellow Bucktail. Sometimes he tied it with a black wool body; other times he used silver tinsel. The fly also worked well when tied with a white bucktail or calftail wing. Later in the season he would fish the MacIntosh flies. Henry tied most of his flies on bronze down eye hooks.

Henry did some guiding both for anglers and deer hunters, and was himself a keen angler, fishing mostly on the St. Mary's but also visiting the Margaree frequently. "He used to keep track of the money he made from fly tying and figured that he needed to have twenty dollars a day to fish the Margaree," says Donnie. Henry kept early-run fish that he caught, but he "didn't like to eat the late-run fish and released most of them," Donnie continues. "I remember my father skinning a fish he caught later in the season one time to see if the taste would improve but it didn't work."

Henry continued tying up until 1965. Some of his flies are on display at the St. Mary's River Interpretation Centre in Sherbrooke, and the jail where he lived and tied his flies still stands as part of the Sherbrooke Village restoration project.

Eric Baylis

Whether because of his reel repair shop, his articles in *SPAWNER* magazine, or his reputation as a master fly tier, Eric Baylis is a well-known figure in the Atlantic Canadian sport-fishing community.

Born in Woodside, near Dartmouth, in 1937, Eric and moved to the Eastern Shore of Nova Scotia when he was six years old. He grew up fishing with his father and brother, who never left him behind. Eric's father, George Baylis, taught him how to tie flies.

Eric joined the army and served six years before returning home where he worked in the parts department at Fairley and Stevens, a local car dealership. All that time he was selling his flies, mostly at the Dartmouth Canadian Tire. He was buying his materials at Phinney's in Halifax, Buck's Tackle in Musquodoboit, and Fred Pettis in Truro, and ordering from Angling Specialties and Fred W. Watson.

Eric used Sportsman cigarette packages to learn new flies; they used to print a trout or salmon fly on their packages. He had a scrapbook full of them at one

The Phantom

Tag:	Fine oval silver tinsel		chartreuse Krystal Flash
Butt:	Fluorescent orange		wound on like floss
Under Body:	Flat silver tinsel	Rib:	Fine oval silver over front
Body:	Rear one-third yellow		body only
	phentex wrapped thin	Wing:	Black squirrel with a few
	over silver with butt of		strands pink Krystal Flash
	fluorescent orange; cen-		mixed in
	tre one-third black os-	Hackle:	Black, two turns
	trich herl; front one-third	Head:	Fluorescent orange

point, mostly English trout flies and traditional salmon flies like the Jock Scott or Dusty Miller. He tied them up using whatever materials he had on hand. They were often successful.

Eric cites Joseph Bates's *Atlantic Salmon Flies and Fishing*, Keith Fulsher and Charles Krom's *Hairwing Atlantic Salmon Flies,* and books by Dick Stewart and Farrow Allen as helpful resources. He has an impressive collection of fly-tying books, but gave up his commercial fly tying in the late 1960s. "I was working full time and then I would come home and stay up until 2 A.M. trying to finish an order. It was too hard," he says. Today Eric ties for himself and friends and donates flies to a variety of sport-fishing groups throughout Atlantic Canada. He is also busy running his reel shop—he is the only person in Nova Scotia repairing fishing reels.

Eric's flies have appeared in a variety of publications, from *SPAWNER* magazine to *Fishing Atlantic Salmon* by Joseph and Pamela Bates. His work has also been seen by millions of Canadians, through the 1998 postage stamp featuring a Cosseboom fly tied by Eric. Eric says the project raised his profile and put his flies in demand.

Eric is a fan of traditional trout and salmon flies and likes tying them. For trout he likes the Dark Montreal and Quebec fly. "The Pink Lady is also a good fly," he says, "but you have to tie it small, #16 or #18, and fish it on a light leader." Eric recommends the Arndilly Fancy for salmon, in sizes #8–10. He likes the look of jungle cock on his salmon flies.

Eric describes the old-fashioned Atlantic Canadian fly-tying style like this: "Well, they made do with what they had. Moose and caribou, deer and bear or squirrel—whatever material they had, they used in their flies. If they were lucky they had tinsel; if they didn't, they would use some tinsel from Christmas decorations."

Eric stresses the creative nature of fly tying, and believes that you don't need five hundred dollars' worth of materials and equipment to tie flies or to fly fish.

Eric likes tying a variety of fly patterns—dries, wets, streamers, and nymphs. He contributed his pattern the Phantom to this book.

The stamp depicting Eric Baylis's Cosseboom fly.

Bill Bryson

Although now retired, Bill once held the job many consider to be the best in Nova Scotia: He was responsible for marketing hunting, fishing and the outdoors for the province. As a result, he has a vast store of knowledge about Nova Scotia flies and fishing as well as some great fishing stories.

Bill was born on a farm in West New Annan and grew up in Truro. Some of his earliest memories are of summers spent fishing the brooks of Colchester County. He began his working career as a campground inspector, but with his knowledge and experience of the outdoors, he eventually began working for the Department of Tourism in the job described above.

Bill began tying flies as a teenager. His barber, a Mr. Jewers from the Eastern Shore, used to keep his fly-tying vice set up in the barbershop and he let Bill tie with it while he was waiting for a haircut. As he improved his tying, Bill began to tie with Ralph Tuttle and other local tiers. After he married, Bill used an empty room by the furnace in his apartment building as his fly-tying space.

One of Bill's favourite early fly-tying references was W. W. Doak's catalogue, and he also found Dick Stewart's *Universal Fly Tying Guide* was also helpful.

Bill tied flies commercially for many years but stopped tying in any volume after a customer ordered twelve gross of one pattern. He still does some custom tying, but mostly ties for his own use or to give to friends. "I always enjoyed tying flies," Bill told me. "I could tie for hours when I got in a rhythm."

Bill favours a sparse fly for both trout and salmon. "Even when I am tying a Blue Upright for trout, I use the minimum amount of hackle I need to float the fly, no more," he says.

Bill generally ties his salmon hooks on Mustad 36890 hooks, with the one exception being his Cosseboom flies, which he always ties on a bronze down eye hook from a #6 right up to a 3/0. "If I was fishing in Newfoundland, I would tie it much smaller, #8 or #10," he clarifies. Bill uses dark green wool for body material on his Cossebooms, and while he uses jungle cock on some of his black flies—like his Dark Edson Tigers—he never uses it on the Cosseboom.

Bill enjoys experimenting with his flies and enjoys tying small flies for both trout and salmon: "The smallest salmon fly I tie is a #20 or #22 Butterfly. I had great luck over the years catching grilse with these small flies. I never had a hook come out."

During his time with the provincial government, Bill guided a who's who of angling writers and publishers, from Lee Wulff and Ernest Schwiebert to the editors of

The Mighty Bryson

Tail:	Yellow hackle tips	Wing:	Black squirrel
Rib:	Flat copper tinsel	Hackle:	Yellow, collared and tied
Body:	Black wool		back

Field and Stream, *Outdoor Life* and *Fly Fisherman*. The person he speaks most fondly of is Lee Wulff, the most important Atlantic salmon angler of the twentieth century and a regular visitor to Nova Scotia, but he remembers the friendliness of all the people he guided.

The Cosseboom is Bill's favourite fly for salmon, and the Muddler Minnow is his first choice for trout. Bill has developed several patterns that have been featured in different publications, including Paul Marriner's *Modern Atlantic Salmon Flies*. One of his patterns, the Mighty Bryson, took Bill's first salmon on the Miramichi.

Ray Buckland

Ray Buckland is a legend on the St. Mary's River as an angler, guide, and fly tier. Born in North Sydney, Nova Scotia, in 1934, Ray moved around the Maritimes with his family for his father's work with Canadian National Telegraph. The family settled in Halifax when Ray started school, and Ray would go on to spend twenty-nine years with the Halifax Fire Department before retiring in 1986 because of damage to his lungs from smoke inhalation. When he retired, Ray and his family moved to the banks of the St. Mary's River.

Ray fished salmon on the La Have, Medway, and Gold rivers, but it wasn't until after he joined the fire department that he began fishing the St. Mary's.

An avid salmon angler, it wasn't long before Ray also began tying flies, picking the craft up on his own. He started tying bugs and bombers for Phil Turner's tackle shop in Smithfield. He was one of the first anglers to fish the General Practitioner on the St. Mary's River; he ordered one from Hardy's in England, and took it apart to see how he could tie his own.

Another pattern Ray helped to popularize on the St. Mary's was the Butterfly. He was tying it on 1/0, 2/0 and 3/0 hooks when everyone else was fishing it in smaller sizes, and he tied the wings off at 90 degrees from the body instead of slanting backward. His Butterfly moved a lot differently in the water than the original.

"For a hundred years, if I live that long, this crumpled book and these broken worn out flies will bring back the clear, wild water and the green shores of a Nova Scotia June, the remoter silences of the deeper forest, the bright camps by twisting pools and tumbling falls, the flash of a leaping trout, the feel of a curved rod and the music of the singing reel."

Albert Bigelow Paine,
The Tent Dwellers (1908)

Butterfly

Butt:	Green and orange floss	Wing:	Goat or calf tail, yellow or white
Body:	Peacock herl		
Rib:	Fine silver tinsel	Hackle:	Brown or yellow

Ray also tinkered with how he tied his bombers—he used to spin deerhair on half the hook and trim it, then add two deerhair wings coming off the body at an angle. Then he would spin more deerhair on to finish the fly. It gave it a different silhouette and showed the salmon something different, which Ray believes to be important. "When I would go to the river I would watch what everyone else was using. Most of the time it was the same basic flies so I would use something completely different," he says.

Visitors to the St. Mary's River Association's Interpretation Centre can view a picture of Ray along with Dr. Harris Miller and Joan and Lee Wulff. They are posing with Ray's record fish, a 31-and-1/4-pounder he caught at Miller's Bank Pool in the early 1980s. "That fish put me in the Hardy Hall of Fame," Ray says. "They also sent me a rod and reel."

Bill Carpan

Bill was born in Toronto in 1945 but returned to Nova Scotia with his parents and settled in Tracadie, near Antigonish. Bill graduated from Mount Allison University and worked as a computer programmer, first in Toronto, then Halifax, and finally in Scotsburn, Nova Scotia, where he retired from Scotsburn Dairy in 2001. Bill and his wife Brenda retired to Stillwater near Bill's beloved St. Mary's River, where they run an angling business, River Magic, which sells flies and fly artwork.

Bill was an avid angler growing up in Tracadie, where he fished with his good friend, the late Bill Strople. One of their favourite spots was the Little Bayfield River, which he often fished with his father while his mother picked fiddleheads.

Bill began fly fishing when he moved back to Halifax to work at Dalhousie University. "I bought a canoe and went trout fishing on a lake near the city one day. I was fishing bait but there was a tremendous mayfly hatch on and the fish wouldn't look at my bait. However another angler, who was fly fishing was catching fish so I resolved to learn how to do it." And learn he did.

With his interest in fly fishing came an interest in tying flies. Bill borrowed Helen Shaw's *Fly Tying* from the library, and taught himself how to tie. Bill still considers the book to be the best introductory guide to fly tying available.

There were a few commercial tiers in Halifax that Bill went to for advice, Heck Wallis and Aubrey Gladwin in particular. Gladwin had a shop in Herring Cove where Bill got most of my supplies, and he also ordered from Herters.

The first formal fly-tying class Bill attended was a course in the early 1990s taught by Mike Crosby and Jim McCoul. "I tied off and on after that but not seriously," Bill

Pink Mystery

Tag:	Extra fine oval silver tinsel	Body:	Pink floss
Tail:	Golden pheasant tippet fibers	Wing:	Teal flank
		Hackle:	Pink
Rib:	Five turns of fine oval silver tinsel	Head:	Black

says. He credits Warren Duncan of Saint John, New Brunswick, for his rebirth as a fly tier. "I attended Warren's fly-tying workshop during the Atlantic Salmon Conclave held on the St. Mary's and came away very impressed with his skill and enthusiasm. He revitalized me as a fly tier." Bill began tying flies commercially after the Conclave and continues to this day.

Although Bill is mainly known for his salmon flies, the fly he selected for this book is a trout pattern he used when he began fly fishing for trout on the Bayfield River. The Pink Mystery has been a popular sea-trout wet fly in Nova Scotia's Antigonish County for many years. The teal wing and tippet tail is characteristic of several British sea-trout flies.

Fly proportions are important to Bill, and one of the biggest problems he sees when teaching fly tying to new tiers is that they don't leave enough room for the head. Bill favours the Partridge Bartleet Supreme for his salmon wet flies but uses Mustad's 90240 for his dries. He weighed twenty-five Mustad 90240 and twenty-five Wilson Dry Fly hooks of the same size on a post office scale, and the Mustad hooks were lighter.

Although Bill believes in tying true to pattern for the flies he sells, he occasionally allows his creative side to run wild at the vice. One of his own patterns, the Moose, was featured in the Spring 2004 issue of the St. Mary's River Association Newsletter. Bill's favourite method of fishing is using dry flies for trout and salmon. His favourite dry flies include the time-tested MacIntosh patterns, which were developed on the St. Mary's, as well as bugs and bombers. "Whichever fly gives the angler more confidence is the one to use," says Bill.

Moyal Conrad

Moyal was born in the community of Brookfield, near Liverpool, Nova Scotia, in 1940 and lived there until he married and moved to the village of Greenfield on the banks of the Medway River.

Growing up fishing trout, it wasn't long before Moyal also began fishing for salmon in the nearby Medway. "Back then the salmon fishing started the first of April, and we used to set a tent up on the banks of the river and leave it up until deer season," recalls Moyal.

Moyal began tying flies when he started salmon fishing. "I used to get some flies from Russell Huey, a local fly tier. His son George and I used to hang around the river, and we started tying flies on our own."

Despite the growing popularity of the dry fly at that time, the first salmon flies he tied were featherwing wet flies, particularly the MacIntosh style tied with a gray squirrel wing, peacock herl body and burnt orange hackle. Lew Freeman, who also lived on the river, tied in the same style. Moyal tied the fly on fairly big hooks, #2 and #4, early in the season, going down to #10–#12 later in the season. "We fished that pattern either wet or dry," says Moyal. "If the fish didn't rise to it when we fished it over them dry, we would fish it as a wet. Usually if they didn't come for one they would come for the other."

Moyal tied commercially for many years, selling flies locally as well as to anglers he guided in his outfitting business. While most of his flies were for trout or salmon, he also tied a fly specifically for harbour pollack. It was a simple pattern, a tinsel body with a few sprigs of white hackle for a wing, but the pollack apparently loved it.

Moyal believes presentation to be just as important as the pattern. "You have to present your fly so the trout or salmon will take it, and that depends on a lot of factors—the time of day, time of year, height of water, colour of the water where you are fishing," he says.

Moyal prefers a fly that is sparsely dressed over a fully dressed one, but, he says, "it depends on conditions. If I am fishing a dry fly in heavy water I want it fairly full so it will float. On quiet water I will use one tied with less material."

Moyal's flies and his outfitting business have been featured in a number of publications. Ken Allen from Maine wrote about his experiences fishing at Moyal's River View Lodge, where he caught a twenty-nine pound salmon on a #10 Blue Charm.

The River View Lodge on the banks of the Medway was a popular destination for anglers and hunters for many years. "I had one sport who fished with me for thirty-five years," recalls Moyal, "and he was planning to come up for his thirty-sixth when he took a heart attack and died." While he continues to guide a few hunters and anglers each season, Moyal closed his lodge a few years ago.

His years spent on the river and in the woods have left Moyal with a keen awareness of what is happening in the natural world. "I go by the seagulls in the river," he says. "When I see them feeding I know that the sea trout are in the river and it's time to go fishing."

John Cosseboom

1885–1935

While there are thousands of hairwing patterns available to modern anglers, a few original flies still have an enormous influence on the sport today. These flies were developed by a handful of early fly tiers who are giants in the history of salmon angling. One of the best tiers was John C. Cosseboom, a poet, newspaper writer, champion fly-caster, and insurance executive who lived in Woonsocket, Rhode Island. Cosseboom made yearly trips to Quebec, New Brunswick and Nova Scotia in pursuit of Atlantic salmon and was a regular visitor to the Margaree River. Several locations have

John Cosseboom, seen here with his wife and a Margaree salmon, was a regular visitor to the Margaree River.

The Cosseboom (original)

Tag:	Embossed silver	Wing:	A small bunch of grey
Tail:	A short piece of olive		squirrel tail
	green floss	Hackle:	Lemon yellow hackle tied
Body:	Olive green floss		in as a beard
Rib:	Oval silver tinsel		

claimed to be the birthplace of the Cosseboom fly, but Joseph Bates Jr. and Pamela Bates Richards put the matter to rest in their book, *Fishing Atlantic Salmon*. In it, they show a photograph of John Cosseboom tying the first Cosseboom fly on the steamer SS *Fleuris* on his way to Anticosti for a fishing trip in 1935. The Cosseboom remains one of the most popular patterns in North America.

Another of John Cosseboom's patterns, the Cosseboom Streamer, was first tied on the Margaree River in 1922 and is one of the earliest examples of a streamers being used for Atlantic salmon.

In his book *The Art of the Atlantic Salmon Fly*, Joseph Bates suggests that the Cosseboom fly suffers from the fly tier's habit of changing the original dressing into numerous different colours, none of which, he feels, match the original in effectiveness. Today there are red, black, silver and yellow variations of the original, but many salmon anglers agree that the original pattern remains the best.

Although he passed away in 1935, John Cosseboom lives on through his flies as well as at the Margaree Salmon Museum, which displays photographs of him on the Margaree with his fishing hat adorned with an assortment of his flies.

Mike Crosby

Born in Halifax in 1955, Mike began fishing trout with his grandmother when he was four and salmon fishing when he was sixteen. His fly-tying career began when he received a fly-tying kit for Christmas at the age of eight or nine. He used the kit's instruction manual and took lessons from a family friend, Ben McCrae. Mike also attended Ron Alcott's workshops on featherwing salmon flies when he visited Halifax.

Mike began tying commercially when he was in school and helped finance his way through a business degree at Dalhousie University. He sold flies to several Halifax stores, including F. M. Harleys, the Mayfly Tackle Shop and Scotia Sports. His love of fishing led him to open Mike's Tackle Shop on Agricola Street in Halifax when he was twenty-seven. Today Mike ties for himself and friends.

Mike likes a well-proportioned, properly sized fly that's not overdressed, and he feels that presentation and size are more important than pattern. He admires the neat, precise flies tied by Warren Duncan of Saint John, New Brunswick, saying that they "look fishy." His favourite flies are the Blue Charm, modified with a green butt, and his own Crosby Special.

Mike's favourite hook for his wet flies is Mustad's 3906, and he likes the bronze down eye and Partridges CS42 for his bombers.

Crosby Special

Tag:	Flat silver	Rib:	Oval silver tinsel
Tail:	Golden pheasant crest	Wing:	Gray squirrel tail
Butt:	Red wool	Hackle:	Peach, collar-style
Body:	In two parts: rear third, fluorescent green floss; the remainder, peacock herl or dark green wool	Cheeks:	Jungle cock
		Head:	Red

Mike was the Atlantic Salmon Federation Fly Tier of the year in 1992 and he also served as a columnist for *Wild Salmon and Steelhead* magazine. Mike is presently working on a book on Atlantic salmon fishing, and while he no longer ties commercially, he is still actively involved in the fly-fishing business. With his partners he operates three salmon lodges on the East Coast: Camp Bonaventure on the Gaspé, and Chute Pool and Hawkes River in Labrador.

Harry Darbee

Modern fly-tying hackle owes its development to the work of American poultry breeders in the 1940s and '50s. One of the leading figures in this development was the late Harry Darbee. Harry and his wife Elsie were commercial fly tiers in the Catskill Mountains of New York state, and as such, they were always searching for good quality feathers. The Darbees have a close connection to Cape Breton, as they fished the Margaree every fall for many years and were well known and liked in the Margaree area. Harry Darbee kept a flock of birds and was constantly experimenting with various crosses. He created his spate fly for fall fishing on the Margaree.

Fly tier, angler and poultry breeder, Harry Darbee left his mark on angling.

Darbee's Spate Fly

Tag:	Oval gold tinsel		nearly to the point of the hook
Tail:	A golden pheasant crest feather	Wing:	A bunch of brown bucktail, reaching to the point of the tail
Body:	Dark brown seal's fur or Polar Bear fur, spun on and slightly picked out	Shoulder:	Fairly wide strips of black and white wood duck, set on both sides of the bucktail and two-thirds as long
Rib:	Medium size oval gold tinsel		
Throat:	Several turns of black hackle, tied on as a collar and puled down, the longest fibres reaching	Head:	Red

Leonard Forsythe

Leonard was born in 1941 in Wolfville and grew up in New Minas. Both Leonard's father and grandfather were avid salmon anglers, and Leonard grew up fishing for trout and salmon on the Gaspereau River near Wolfville, where he also first caught a salmon. As Leonard recalls it, there were a lot of gaspereau running in the river and he was sent down the river to catch some for his grandfather, who would smoke them. "They were trying to get rid of me," laughs Leonard, "so they could fish salmon." Leonard was using a bamboo rod and a reel that had no drag, so to keep the line from running out he took a turn around his finger. He would cast into the river, hook a gaspereau and flip it onto the bank. On one cast he felt a strong pull, and a bright salmon jumped at the end of the line. His father and grandfather saw the fish jump and began shouting to play the fish, but Leonard couldn't get the line off his finger. The tug of war continued until the fish eventually broke off—but not before cutting Leonard's finger to the bone. Later, his father and grandfather chided him about losing his first salmon: "You've seen us play fish; you should know you can't hold them," they both said. When Leonard explained what had happened and showed them his finger, his grandfather berated Leonard's father for giving the boy such poor gear. "The next day my father came home with a new reel, a condex," says Leonard.

Leonard's father and grandfather both tied flies, so he grew up watching them at the vice and was soon tying his own flies. He also received some lessons in fly tying from well-known Annapolis Valley commercial fly tier Stan Wagstaff. "He was my mentor," recalls Leonard.

Leonard tied commercially for several years, selling flies at Bishop's Taxi Stand and Sports Shop in Wolfville. He was mostly tying salmon flies—the Silver Grey Bomber, Cosseboom, Ross Special, MacIntosh and a couple of his own patterns, Len's Special and the Fred Forsythe Special, named after his grandfather.

Leonard eventually joined the Department of Fisheries and Oceans and worked in the fish culture section for thirty years, retiring as manager of the Margaree Fish Culture Centre in 1997.

Leonard likes to tie his wet flies fairly sparsely, and prefers his Len's Special, which he describes as a modified Dusty Miller. In high water he turns to the Fred Forsythe Special, in larger sizes, from 1/0 to 2/0. Leonard is also a big fan of the MacIntosh-style dry fly. "It's hard to beat the MacIntosh," he says as he shows me an impressive selection of dry flies. He prefers it on a larger hook, usually a #2 Mustad 94840: "You

Fred Forsythe Special

Body:	Flat silver tinsel with middle section of black floss	Wing:	Black bear
		Cheeks:	Jungle cock
Rib:	Oval silver tinsel	Throat:	Guinea fowl

need a big fly for big water," says Leonard. "I believe that anglers are using a fly that is too small most of the time."

Leonard lives on the banks of the Margaree River, Nova Scotia's premiere salmon river, so he is intimately familiar with the river and its fish. His favourites for the river include the Ross Special and Mickey Finn in the fall.

Leonard says a good fly is tough, and he believes colour combinations and presentation are also important.

Living near the base of the Cape Breton Highlands, Leonard often travels to the lakes there for brook trout. His favourite trout fly is a small orange bug, tied with a white deerhair body, white calftail and orange hackle. He ties it on a #8 Mustad 9672 hook and fishes it wet or dry. Early in the spring when the water is cold, Leonard's favourite is an old-time streamer, the Bumblepuppy.

While Leonard no longer ties commercially, he continues to tie for family and friends and donates flies to various organizations. He also teaches a few fly-tying classes now and then. Although Leonard spent his working life in sport fish management, he has also made major contributions to sport-fish conservation in Nova Scotia. He has served as president of the Margaree Salmon Association and on the executive of the Aquatic Development Association of Margaree, and he has received numerous awards for his conservation work, including a place on the Atlantic Salmon Federation's Roll of Honour, the Margaree Salmon Association's Cormack Award and the Marshall Kaiser award from the Nova Scotia Department of Agriculture and Fisheries.

Lew Freeman

1913–1990

"Earlier, during our drive over from Sunnybrook to Greenfield, Hal told me that so adept was Lew in the use of one hand that he should have been a surgeon. Now, fascinated, I watched Lew's amazing dexterity in attaching one-handed the salmon fly to the end of Hal's gut leader, and agreed wholeheartedly with Hal's assessment. With the butt of the rod firmly tucked into the armpit of his amputated arm, Lew whipped the fly on as if by magic. Just a couple of flicks of agile fingers and the trick was done."

Jack Dowell, The Look-Off Bear *(1974)*

Lew Freeman was born in Greenfield, Queens County, and lived there all his life. He lost his right arm in a sawmill accident when he was nineteen but soon learned to use his left hand. He worked as a timber scaler for Bowaters, but he was also an entrepreneur who bought timber, guided, and trapped.

Lew's son Bryant (see profile in Chapter 2) says that while they fished with wet flies in the high water at the start of the season, when the weather warmed up he and Lew would tie on a Medway Special and leave it on until the end of the season. The fly is similar to the MacIntosh, except, Bryant points out, the fly has a tail

Medway Special

Tail:	Golden pheasant tippets	Wing:	Red squirrel
Body:	Peacock herl	Hackle:	Toucan yellow, tied full

and the hackle is tied on heavier. Bryant and Lew used saddle hackle instead of neck hackle for the flies, favouring the softer hackle over the stiff—the stiff hackle made the fly ride too high in the water. The Medway series of flies was tied with a variety of hackle colours, ranging from badger and orange to brown and white.

Mike Parker, in his excellent book *Guides of the North Woods*, recounts a conversation he had with Lew about his time spent guiding. In the interview, Lew outlines his experience with flies:

> In the old days before fishermen started making their own flies, all the salmon flies we had came from England. The Hardy flies were the ones people wanted, and the standard patterns were Green Highlander, Silver Grey, Jock Scott, Durham Ranger, Black Dose. Those were the standard wet flies. Then they started with dry flies. They were bushy big-winged flies, and the standard patterns were Cinnamon Sedge, Pink Lady, Wickham's Fancy, Brown Hackles and Grey Hackles. When I was tying flies there were two of us involved then, my brother Emerson and I. I used to make the body part of the fly. He would put the wing on and then I'd put the hackle on. Today, I make my own dry flies. With my brother gone, my wife cuts the squirrel tail off the bone and holds it to the hook. Then I make two turns with a little glue and I'm all set.

John Hart

John lives along the banks of his beloved Margaree River, where he was born in 1955. When he is not actively working to conserve the river and its salmon through his involvement with the Margaree Salmon Association, you will likely find him either fishing, guiding, or tying flies. John fished trout as a boy and began fly fishing in 1987 when an Atlantic salmon conclave was hosted on the river by the Margaree Salmon Association. He enjoys all types of fly fishing, "whether it is fishing with a seven-foot three-weight for trout or a fourteen-foot spey rod for fall salmon," he says.

John's interest in fly fishing soon led to an interest in fly tying. His aunt, Frances Hart, gave him some fly-tying equipment about fourteen years ago. He picked up some pointers from Ben Edwards, a fly tier from Maine who fished nearby. John kept Edwards supplied with squirrel tails, and Edwards would give him fly-tying lessons.

The first book John used was Dick Stewart's *Universal Fly Tying Guide*. He later found Bates's and Poul Jorgensen's books to be useful. John is a big fan of the late Poul Jorgenson and remembers fondly time spent with him on the Margaree.

The two met when John had been fishing and was heading back to his car.

Hospitality

Tag:	Oval silver tinsel	Wing:	Electric blue flashabou
Body:	Black wool or floss		topped with black squirrel
Rib:	Oval silver tinsel	Collar:	Silver Doctor blue

"I met a fellow sitting in a lawn chair under a tree," says John. "We struck up a conversation and he asked me if I tied my own flies. I told him that I did and he replied, 'Perhaps you've used one of my books.' I replied, 'I may have, and you are?' 'Poul Jorgensen,' he replied. I was thrilled to meet him and his fishing companion, Floyd Franke, a fly-casting instructor at the Wulff Fly Fishing School. I invited them back to the house and they ended up parking their camper in my yard for several days."

Jorgenson and Franke met one of John's neighbours while fishing the Hart Pool near John's house, and the neighbour told them that he had raised five fish with a no-name black-and-blue fly. "That evening when they came to the house, we broke out the fly-tying gear and they attempted to come up with a version of it, which they did," says John. "After some discussion on what to call the new fly, they decided that due to the way they had been treated during their time on the Margaree, they would call it the Hospitality. It has accounted for a few fish since then. The first person to hook a fish with it was Leon Gorman, president of L.L. Bean, who caught four fish on the Margaree in three days on that fly." John told me that Jorgensen later sent him a signed copy of one of his books, and a fly.

Although John doesn't consider himself a commercial fly tier, he ties some custom orders and also sells some flies through the Margaree Salmon Museum. He also guides, mostly on the Margaree but also on Middle River; he has even guided some anglers from Louisiana who wanted to go ice fishing for smelt on the Bras d'Or Lakes.

John likes a durable, neat-looking fly. He's fortunate to have his Aunt Francis nearby; as curator of the Margaree Salmon Museum, she has seen thousands of ties and knows what makes a good one. She serves as John's quality control.

John has taught fly tying at local schools as well as special events like the Fishing Ladies Only Weekend, held annually on the Margaree, and the Becoming an Outdoor Woman event.

John's favourite patterns for salmon are the Blue Charm, Undertaker, Allie's Shrimp, and the Hospitality. For trout, he likes small Muddler Minnows with a silver tinsel body or small dry flies, such as a Humpy or Royal Coachman.

Waldo Hendsbee

1914–1996

Waldo Hendsbee was born in the community of Isaacs Harbour, Guysborough County, in 1914 and moved with his family to Argyle, Guysborough County, as a boy. When Waldo was twelve

Waldo's Five Cent Fly

Tail:	Red hackle
Body:	Black floss
Wing:	Squirrel tail, very sparse

Hackle: Few strands of black hackle tied as a beard

his father died, and he left school at an early age to support the family. He would later go to work in a gold mine at Pickle Crow, Ontario, for several years. He eventually returned home to work in the woods, and later bought a gravel truck that he operated himself.

Waldo fished trout throughout his life but did not take up salmon fishing until he was in his fifties. However, his son Delbert says that "once he started salmon fishing, he lived on the river." Later in life Waldo suffered from ill health that forced the amputation of first one leg, then the other. After the first amputation, Waldo kept fishing and had Delbert take him to Cummingers Pool on the St. Mary's River on his four-wheeler, where he fished off the back of the machine. Waldo fished this way for four years until he lost the second leg and passed away three months later. Delbert attributes some of his father's success as an angler to his great eyesight. "He could read water and see fish better than anyone."

Waldo started tying flies when he took up salmon fishing and continued until just before he died. "He tied 4400 flies the winter before he died," Delbert says, "and he used the same fly-tying gear from when he started until the end." Delbert still ties on his father's old vice.

Waldo gave his flies away, many of them in the fly wallets his wife Minnie made for him. Waldo could not read or write, and learned patterns from other anglers on the river. According to Delbert, "If someone gave him a fly he took it home and copied it." Waldo was a good friend of Ted Mansfield from Halifax and they often fished together. Ted was also a good fly tier and Delbert says his father got a lot of patterns from his friend.

"He never hesitated spending money on his fly tying," Delbert says of his father. "He always bought the best materials he could."

Waldo was a big fan of Fenwick rods and of both Hardy and J. W. Young reels; Delbert still fishes with his father's Marquis and Pridex reels. Delbert also showed me his collection of flies tied by Waldo. "He liked little black flies," says Delbert.

Eric Jefferson

Eric was born in Bridgewater, Nova Scotia, in 1952 but grew up in Halifax. An avid angler and fly tier, Eric's professional life is also centred around sport fish. He has been employed as a technician with the Department of Fisheries and Oceans since 1972, working on Atlantic salmon conservation and enhancement in Nova Scotia. Eric grew up fly fishing with his father,

Jock Scott-Hairwing

Tag:	Silver tinsel	Hackle:	Black hackle palmered over the black floss
Tail:	Golden pheasant topped with red schlappen	Throat:	Guinea hen
Butt:	Ostrich herl	Wing:	Grey squirrel, red, yellow and blue polar bear, Russian brown squirrel
Body:	Rear half: golden yellow floss butted with black ostrich herl and veiled with floss; front half: black floss	Sides:	Jungle cock
		Cheeks:	Kingfisher blue hackle tips
		Hackle:	Yellow hackles
Rib:	Fine oval silver		

fishing for trout right from the beginning. He began tying flies around 1972, borrowing his uncle's gear to tie up a few flies. He used to drop into the May Fly Tackle Shop and talk to the people there about flies and fly tying. Later on, he took a course from Heck Wallace.

Eric is a master fly tier who can turn out any fly pattern, although he is perhaps best known for his dry flies. "I am passionate about dry flies for salmon," Eric said. "I tie a dry Cosseboom that has caught a lot of fish for me over the years. The first salmon I caught on the La Have River was on a dry Cosseboom in 1965. That fly accounted for seven fish that week."

Eric believes that proportion is the most important factor in tying dry flies for salmon: "The fly has to float correctly on the water," he says. Eric uses a variety of hooks for his flies but generally selects Wilson light wire hooks or Mustad 94840s for his dry flies.

Eric's friend Brian Sweeney once caught thirty-two salmon on one of Eric's bugs, a testament to the durability of his flies: "You don't want them to come apart," says Eric. "I use head cement right through the process, from laying down a thread base for the body to lie on, to attaching the wing. If you use cement all the way along, the material on the fly can't go anywhere or come undone."

Eric first tied commercially for Frank Harley, who operated a gun and fishing tackle shop, and he continues to tie commercially for Fishing Fever in Halifax and private customers. He also donates flies to conservation groups such as the Nova Scotia Salmon Association, and the Sackville and La Have River Associations.

Eric dyes his own material in order to get the colours he wants for his flies. While he ties bugs and bombers, he is also a fan of traditional dry flies such as the Wulff and MacIntosh patterns for salmon. He ties them in a variety of sizes right down to #12 and #14.

Albert Jenkins

Just as anglers in Newfoundland demand Smokey Ball's bombers, anglers on Cape Breton Island consider Albert Jenkins' bombers to be the gold standard as far as deerhair bombers go.

Albert's Surface Stonefly

Body:	Green or charcoal deer-hair spun on and trimmed small	Wing:	Green or charcoal buck-tail. Tied in and flared at the head to form a post
Hackle:	Golden badger hackle		

Albert was born in Glace Bay in 1947 and lived there for much of his life while he worked in the coal mines of Cape Breton. He began tying flies thirty-five years ago when he started fishing salmon in North River. "I used to stay with a fishery officer when I was fishing down there, Eric MacAskill, and Eric taught me how to tie my first fly," Albert says, adding that he started tying deerhair bugs right from the start. Albert's bugs are well known in Cape Breton for their durability and effectiveness.

Albert's favourite hook for his bugs and bombers used to be the Mustad's 38941, but it was discontinued. Now he uses the Mustad 9672, but his favourite is the Partridge CS42, which he calls a beautiful hook.

While Albert is best known for his bugs and bombers, he is constantly experimenting with new patterns and fly-tying styles. Two of his latest patterns are his Surface Stonefly and his Bullet or Small Head Muddler.

For his Stonefly, Albert adapted the work of Mack Strathdee, who runs a local fly shop and ties a Surface Stonefly using a bent pin as a post for the hackle. Albert modified it by using spun deerhair for the body and adding a bucktail wing. When he tightens down on the butt of the bucktail, it flares it up and he uses it as the post for the parachute hackle.

Albert is a big fan of the Muddler Minnow, which he ties with very small heads. They are pretty much the only fly he fishes for fall salmon on the Margaree.

Albert tied commercially for over thirty years, but he seldom sold his flies for cash, preferring to barter for sporting goods—everything from rifles to rods and even golf clubs.

Albert used to teach fly-tying courses in Glace Bay. "Every winter I would teach ten or twelve people. I always enjoyed passing on what I knew," he says. But 2004–2005 was the first winter in thirty-five years that Albert didn't tie flies. Instead, he spent the winter in Florida. As soon as he returned to his home in Margaree, he was back at the vice, tying up to thirty-six bombers a day.

"That's nothing," he laughs. "The most I ever tied in one day was 147 bombers. My hands were sore after that."

Tom Lee

Tom was born in 1966 in Halifax, where he works today as a stockbroker. He remembers fishing with his grandfather when he was four years old. "All I caught was perch and chubs," recalls Tom, "but I loved it."

Maple Syrup Nymph

Tail:	Yellow calf tail or goathair	chenille, number 41 beige
Body:	Size 2 Danville rayon	(tied on thick)

By the time he was six, Tom was fly fishing and tying flies under the guidance of his grandfather, and although he continued to fish while going to school and university, he got away from the fly tying. It wasn't until he was twenty-one or twenty-two that he got back into it, after reading an article on fly tying in *Fly, Rod and Reel*.

Tom credits several people with helping him develop his fly tying, including Brian Sweeney, his mentor, with whom he took a fly-tying course, and Reg Baird, another well-known Nova Scotia angler and tier who has influenced Tom.

Tom began tying commercially around the year 2000, and markets his flies as Lee Family Flies. He sells his flies in shops from Maine to Nova Scotia and also does custom tying. His production varies from one to two hundred dozen a year, and he still enjoys tying; he finds it very relaxing after a day at the office.

Tom is also a keen angler, especially for trout. He enjoys salmon fishing, but since most of it now occurs in the fall it conflicts with his second favourite outdoor activity: hunting for grouse and woodcock.

Tom's go-to trout pattern is the Muddler Minnow, and he also likes the Haystack series of flies and the Maple Syrup Nymph, on which he has even caught Salmon. In terms of his best sellers, the Mickey Finn and Coneheads are popular, and he sees a resurgence in patterns such as the Edson Tiger.

Tom ties many of his Nymph patterns on Mustad 3665A hooks, while he prefers the 9672 for his Streamers.

He believes the pattern can be very important: "I have seen an Edson Tiger outfish a Muddler Minnow eight to one," he says. "Both were fished the same way, trolled behind a canoe, so in that case the fly made the difference. Other times presentation may make the difference."

Alex Libbus

1911–1993
Alex was born and raised in Sydney, Nova Scotia. He worked as a barber before joining the Royal Canadian Air Force in World War Two. When he returned home, he opened a restaurant, Alex's Lunch, and later a tavern, The Steel City, the first in Sydney. He sold the business in the 1960s and, as his son Isaac says, "spent the rest of his life hunting and fishing." Alex's reputation as an angler is well documented on Cape Breton Island. "He fished twelve months of the year," Isaac says. "Early in the winter he would start spearing eels, then turn to fishing smelt all winter. In the spring he would begin fishing trout in April and then turn to salmon in the summer. He also fished mackerel, cod and tuna—you name it, he fished for it."

Libbus Special

Tag:	Flat silver tinsel		Rib:	Oval silver tinsel
Butt:	Rose-coloured floss		Wing:	Mallard flank topped with
Tail:	Golden pheasant crest			golden pheasant crest
	followed by second butt of		Throat:	Golden pheasant tippets
	peacock herl		Collar:	Peacock herl
Body:	Flat silver tinsel			

When the opportunity to take a fishing or hunting trip arose, Alex never hesitated. Isaac remembers hearing stories of his father being visited by friends in the barber shop while he was working. One of his buddies would come in and tell him he was going fishing or hunting. Alex would even up the hair of whoever was in the chair and tell him, "That's good enough—come back tomorrow and I'll finish it."

Alex was a good friend of Joe Aucoin and they often fished together. Alex's fly-tying style reflects Aucoin's influence, with golden pheasant used to veil the wings the flies. Although he never tied commercially, Alex gave flies away to friends or anglers he met on the river. He tied every morning if he wasn't going fishing.

Alex preferred wet flies with jungle cock, but he kept up with the times, as evidenced by the boxes of bugs and bombers he tied later in life. He also had a good selection of books, ranging from Edson Leonard's *Flies* to Bates's books on streamers and salmon flies. He kept detailed notes on his fly tying and made little books of typed fly patterns and instructions for dyeing materials. Isaac believes he used them in the fly-tying classes he gave in Sydney over the years.

Alex built a camp in Margaree Forks in 1957 and for the rest of his life fished the Margaree River, as well as the Baddeck and Middle rivers. He preferred the lower areas of the river and his legacy lives on in the Libbus Pool, named in his honour by local fisheries officer Dave Carroll.

Alex guided hunters and anglers, and his exploits were legendary. He didn't usually fish when he was guiding; he would sit on the bank while his sports fished the pool. Eventually one of them would say, "Show us how it's done, Libbus," and he would go through and catch a fish. The secret to his success, according to Isaac, is that he knew the river, and never took his eyes off the water. And his flies fished well.

Isaac still has his father's fly boxes, and one of the flies Alex left behind was a pattern unrecognizable to many experienced tiers. For the purposes of this book, it has been christened the Libbus Special. It retains many Joe Aucoin touches, such as a golden pheasant crest.

Rick MacDonald

Rick is a well-known fly tier on Cape Breton Island, and his flies are always in demand among savvy trout and salmon anglers. He was born in Sydney in 1949 and spent his working life in various parts of the Sydney steel plant, from the open hearth to the coke ovens. He worked a lot of back shift, and he would tie flies at all hours, whenever he came home from work.

Rick has been tying flies for forty-five years. He was taught by his father and some of his father's friends, like Alex Libbus (profiled above). When he was learning, very few people were selling flies commercially; anglers either ordered flies from England or tied them themselves. Rick says that there was a "fraternity of fly tiers" in Cape Breton who tied out of necessity. "You could buy trout flies, but they were cheap things that sold for five cents apiece and they soon fell apart." Rick started tying hairwings because he couldn't afford to buy featherwings. He also started experimenting with different fly patterns for both trout and salmon and kept a log book to record their effectiveness.

As a commercial tier, Rick believes there are two types of flies: ones to catch anglers and ones to catch fish. "The fisherman flies look great in your hat," laughs Rick. He mostly ties standard patterns that have stood the test of time, but he is constantly modifying them to improve their fish-catching abilities.

He puts one wing on the Royal Coachman, for instance, instead of the usual two. He ties it a lot faster and the fish don't seem to mind! But despite their effectiveness, no one seems to want to buy the modified fly.

Rick believes that the quality of the fly-tying material available to the average fly tier has improved over time. "Today there are better materials such as genetic hackle by Hoffman and Whiting. When I started tying, in the late fifties and early sixties, we had to order most of our material from Veniards in England. Joe Aucoin used to sell some material in New Waterford, and we bought some stuff there as well." Rick thinks back fondly on the quality of the old hooks. "The Gaelic Supreme was the standard for salmon; it was a beautiful hook, all handmade." Mustad hooks began to replace the old hooks as the Mustad 36890 became widely available.

Rick also remembers the old-style flies he used to tie. "When I started tying there were no bugs and bombers or Muddlers. The Cosseboom and MacIntosh were popular patterns as well as standard English patterns such as the Jock Scott, Silver Gray and Green Highlander."

Rick does not believe in rules for fly tying. He is constantly creating new fly patterns for Cape Breton trout and salmon, many of them based on what Rick

Bras d'Or Creeper

Hook:	Mustad 3582, #6-10	Hackle:	Hackle to match body, palmered and trimmed on top
Thread:	Black		
Antennae:	Red squirrel		
Beak:	Pheasant body feather	Rib:	Oval gold tinsel
Body:	Brown, green or orange dubbing	Eyes:	Black barbells or melted mono
Back:	Clear plastic strip		

sees in the water and inside fish. "I always look at the stomach contents of fish I keep. Why use a red fly if they are eating brown caddis that day?" The Bras d'Or Creeper, included here, is Rick's attempt at imitating a saltwater shrimp, a major part of the diet of brook, brown and rainbow trout in Cape Breton's Bras d'Or Lakes. But Rick says that "some standards can't be improved on—for example, the Mickey Finn. No other combination works as well as that red and yellow wing, and I tried them all."

Rick is also a keen observer of how his flies look and move in the water. He once lay on the bottom of a pool in the river and breathed through a piece of garden hose while a friend cast flies and drifted them through the pool so that Rick could study their size and motion.

While Rick is a long-time Atlantic salmon angler, his favourite fish is the brook trout. He often fishes a cast of three flies for trout; the point fly is usually a Muddler, Leech or a minnow imitation with a Dark Montreal on the drop and a Queen of the Waters on the dib or bob. Rick is firm believer in selective harvest for trout and releases any trout under ten inches. He is also a fan of brown trout, and the largest he has caught to date was nine and three-quarter pounds.

Rick is still ties traditional featherwing salmon flies in addition to his commercial tying and custom orders. He also finds time to teach fly-tying classes in Sydney during the winter, a job he enjoys. "It's fun passing on what I know." The first thing he teaches his students is that a fly should be sparse and well-proportioned, especially if it is going to be sold.

In comparing the flies he ties for himself and those he plans to sell, Rick says, "If you are tying for yourself, then please yourself. When I am tying to sell, I tie by the book; people deserve to get the correct pattern they ordered, but the flies I fish with are usually much simpler."

Dan and Danny MacIntosh

The St. Mary's River in Guysborough County has long been known both as the home of big salmon and the birthplace of the MacIntosh salmon fly. Dan MacIntosh (1906–1969) was a legend on the St. Mary's River and his legend lives on in the fly that bears his name.

Dan was born in Stillwater, along the banks of the St. Mary's River, and except for time spent working during the winters on the dockyards in Halifax, he lived there all his life. Along with his five brothers, Dan was a master angler and guide. He supplemented his guiding income with work in the woods. His ability to catch salmon was legendary, as was his casting prowess; he was reported to cast with such force that he often broke rods. His son, Danny Jr., lives close to the family home in Stillwater and continues the family fly-fishing and fly-tying tradition. Danny believes that most sports writers failed to understand that his father approached fishing differently than they did: "Most days when he went to the river he was fishing for food for the family," Danny says. Dan and his wife had eleven children, and provid-

The Original MacIntosh

Wing: Local red squirrel   Hackle: Brown
Body: None

ing for them was not an easy matter. Dan fished hard and didn't play with his fish. He brought them in quickly, gaffed them and brought them home for supper.

Danny acknowledges that his father was a powerful caster and suggests that part of his fishing success was due to his ability to fish lies that other anglers couldn't reach. Dan often made his own rods. "He would go to the woods and cut a rock or sugar maple, split it and work it, first with the axe, then the plane and finally a piece of glass until he had it the way he wanted," says Danny. The rods were two piece. "He would use a rifle cartridge for the ferrule, some haywire for the guides, and he was in business." Dan used an old brass reel someone gave him. He often bartered for equipment.

Dan began tying flies as a young boy, using local materials such as bucktail and squirrel tail. He sold flies commercially, and when his six sons were old enough, they also began tying flies. "It was mostly us boys who tied during the summer; our father was too busy guiding on the river," Danny says.

Dan guided many famous visitors to the St. Mary's, including Babe Ruth and Lee Wulff. In *The Atlantic Salmon*, Wulff credits Dan MacIntosh with teaching him how to land a salmon by grasping it at the base of the tail. Wulff popularized this technique and today tailing has replaced netting and gaffing as a technique for landing salmon. Dan often guided anglers staying at Kirk's Cabins and the Sherbrooke Hotel. During the fall he guided deer hunters at Bill Parks Sunset Camp in Sheet Harbour.

Dan "lived on the river during the season. I can remember him sleeping there," says Danny. "He studied the fish. He watched where they were tending and when they moved. He could tell the weather by them; if they were restless and moving he knew the weather was changing. He could smell them. I saw him stand by the river many times and say, 'There are no fish here today.' He could sense them."

Danny has inherited his father's salmon sense and is well known as one of the best anglers on the St. Mary's River. Unfortunately, the river has fallen on hard

"Hence, it was my good fortune as a novice salmon fisherman on the Margaree to become associated with a group of dedicated anglers, guests of the Harts at North East Margaree. 'Salmon' was the language spoken around the Harts' table morning, noon and far into the night. These men were generous with knowledge of the basic skills and in particular of their understanding of the river. Even so, my apprenticeship lasted four years before my first silvery prize was tailed, a bright salmon from Harts's Pool."

James T. Grey, *Handbook for the Margaree* (1987)

times in recent years, and except for a short catch-and-release season in 2004, has been closed to salmon angling.

Dan would fish the MacIntosh fly as both a wet and a dry. If he was fishing it as a wet fly, he used only a few turns of hackle. The floating version was slightly more heavily hackled. Dan intended the fly to fish in the film on the surface of the water. It was dressed with a homemade floatant of parawax and naptha. "He didn't want it to ride high in the water," Danny says. "He believed that if it was riding high on the water then the salmon would push it out of the way when he rose. The bulge of water would push it away and the fish would miss it."

Dan tied on a variety of vices including a Thompson, as well as ones that his brothers made while working in the shipyards in Halifax. The family would get their hooks at Jack Anderson's store in Sherbrooke and some materials from Thompson and Sutherlands in New Glasgow. Danny can remember getting some mail-order materials from National Specialty.

Danny and his brothers mostly tied squirrel and bucktail patterns. "No one fished small flies back then. The smallest fly I remember my father ever using was a #2." These days Danny seldom ties flies any larger than #2 and will go as small as a #10.

Danny spent some time living with his aunt Laura MacInnis and her husband in Musquodoboit while he was growing up. "She learned how to tie flies from Dan and her other brothers, and she tied commercially for years," Danny says. "She sold flies in several stores in Halifax."

While Dan fished with his own flies, he also used ones he received from anglers he guided. Some of the more popular patterns included the Lady Amherst, Silver Gray and Green Highlander. When Dan fished, the season began in early April when the large three-sea winter salmon entered the river. Anglers used big wet flies for early season fishing but switched to smaller flies later in the season. Most of the early fishing was carried out using riverboats, and Danny acknowledges that his father and Doc Silver were the two best boatmen on the river. "He could fish with one hand and handle the boat with the other. It allowed him to cover a lot of water." Most of Dan's fishing was done close to home: "From the Ford to Archibald's Brook, he knew every rock," says Danny.

Gordie MacKinnon

Few fly tiers are as enthusiastic about their tying as Gordie. Born in Sydney Mines in 1945, he retired from his job as an electrician in the coal mines in 1999. He began tying flies with his friend, the late Jim Purcell. "Jim and I fished together," recalls Gordie. "I fished bait while Jim fly fished. I could match his catch early in the season but as the water warmed up he would out-fish me with flies so I became interested in fly fishing." In the mid seventies, his interest turned to tying his own flies. He never took a course, but he sometimes had help from Allan MacLean, who also worked at the mines.

Gordie's Shrimp

Antennae: Orange hackle	Hackle: Orange palmered over
Abdomen: Orange chenille	body and trimmed
Eyes: Black bead chain	Shell Back: Orange ribbon
Body: Orange floss	Rib: Orange thread

Gordie was soon tying flies commercially, and when he retired he formed a company, Mac's Flies, through which he sells trout and salmon flies, smelt and mackerel gear and fly-tying material. He uses standard Mustad hooks such as the 36890, 9672 and 3399A for most of his salmon, trout and streamers or bugs, although he will tie on special hooks if clients provide them. At one time Gordie tied flies for large retailers such as Canadian Tire, but when they switched to a barcode pricing system they required that each fly be individually coded, making the price too prohibitive for a small business and ending his large-scale tying venture.

Gordie says that these days, people are asking him for the standard salmon patterns—Cosseboom, Blue Charm and the bug. But his favourite, without question, is the orange General Practitioner, which he calls a great fly for Cape Breton. Gordie fished trout for many years before starting to fish for salmon, but when he started, he fished salmon almost exclusively. Only when he retired did he have the time to start fishing for trout again, and then much of his interest was focused on the Bras d'Or Lakes, Cape Breton's inland sea. "I have had great luck fishing for brook trout in the lakes with the Mickey Finn as well as the Orange Shrimp. The shrimp I tie is a modification of Lester the Lobster. The pattern called for a back of orange surveyor's tape but I found that it didn't hold up well so I substituted ribbon and found it much tougher. I also used bead chain for eyes."

Gordie likes a durable fly that won't come apart. "Some of the imported flies look good," he says, "but many of them don't hold up to a lot of fishing, so there are always anglers who come to local tiers [for] the quality and durability they demand." Gordie credits Dick Stewart's *Universal Fly Tying Guide* and the complete set of Stewart and Allen's fly-tying books as being a great source of patterns and an important reference for him.

Allan MacLean

Allan was born in Florence on Cape Breton Island in 1939, and grew up there before leaving to join the Canadian Air Force. Later he returned home and began working for DEVCO (the Cape Breton Development Corporation) in the coal wash plant, where he remained until retiring. Like many of his friends, Allan grew up fishing for trout. "Salmon was out of our league," recalls Allan. "It was a rich man's sport at that time."

Allan's fly tying began when he couldn't purchase the patterns he wanted locally. The only place he could buy salmon flies was at the Woolco department store in Sydney River, which carried flies tied by John Roberts from Montreal, a few popular patterns like the Ross Special, Blue Charm Cosseboom and some Black Bears, in two sizes.

Allan was interested in experimenting with new patterns, and realized that if he wanted different flies, he would have to tie them himself. After reading an instructional fly-tying book from Herters, he ordered a vice from them, a Herters Model 9, which he used until he wore it out, switching to a Thompson and then a Regal.

Allan began tying flies commercially in 1963 and used to tie about five thousand flies a year. Today he continues to tie flies commercially for custom orders and friends.

His favourite fly for both trout and salmon is the General Practitioner. "In smaller sizes I use it for summer fishing on the North River, while in the fall I go to a larger size," he says. He continues to tie twelve to fourteen dozen General Practitioners every year and ties them on double hooks. He has also come up with several of his own patterns, including the Mac series, which he ties in a variety of colours.

Allan has ordered his material from a variety of sources, including Doak's and George Morris. "George used to run a mail order fly-tying material business in New Brunswick before he moved back to Cape Breton. You know, it was George who brought the bug and bomber to Cape Breton," Allan adds. "Only a few people were fishing them at that time and they were trying to keep it quiet because they were so successful."

Allan favours Doak's salmon hooks for most of his flies, and finds the Mustad 36890 too heavy and dull for most applications. He prefers a small eye on a hook; "That way you don't have to worry about the line slipping around the eye on you."

The most useful books for Allan were Jack Dennis's *Western Fly Tying Manual*, Volumes I and II, and Bates's books on salmon and streamers. He also cites Poul Jorgensen's, Eric Leiser's, and Randall Kaufman's books as helpful.

Allan spends a lot of time fishing and tying flies for trout, especially Nymphs and the Hare's Ear Nymph for Cape Breton. He used to tie down to size 22, but the smallest he ties now is a #16. Allan brings different tying styles to his flies depending on the pattern. "I like to use jungle cock on some of my flies such as the Blue Charm, but the Cosseboom and Ross Special don't need it. On some flies I like to use the large jungle cock eyes in the Aucoin style." One of Allan's innovations is his use of chenille as a head on his Muddlers rather than the traditional spun deerhair.

Blue Mac

Tag:	Oval tinsel	Wing:	Red squirrel
Butt:	Fluorescent blue floss	Hackle:	Light blue palmered over body
Tail:	Golden pheasant crest		
Body:	Black wool	Throat:	Guinea fowl
Ribs:	Oval silver	Cheeks:	Jungle cock

Allan likes to use steelhead patterns for Atlantic salmon, especially in the fall. "Most of them are fairly bright—red, orange and yellow—all favourite colours for our fall salmon flies." Allan is also a fan of the Trude-style flies, with wings tied low on the body of the fly, and he ties most of his flies fairly sparse: "When you tie them that way, the material in the wing and hackle moves when you are fishing them, while a fly tied with too much material is dead in the water."

Allan has been a frequent contributor to *SPAWNER* magazine over the years. His first article was about traditional salmon flies tied with moosehair wings, and other articles have been about topics ranging from the Margaree Salmon Museum to Joe Aucoin and some of Allan's own experimental fly patterns.

Jim McCoul

Born in 1946, Jim grew up in Truro, Nova Scotia, and remembers fishing for trout as a boy. He began fly fishing in his early teens when a neighbour, Art Langille, taught him the basics. "The fly tying came later," Jim told me. "I bought a vice and a copy of Poul Jorgensen's *Fly Tying Guide*, and I taught myself."

Jim's interest in traditional Atlantic salmon flies came after he attended two workshops given by Ron Alcott. "I also read a lot on it, including the books by Kelson and Pryce-Tannatt. Everyone ties a little different, so you pick up different tips on how to handle material."

Jim has obviously mastered the craft, receiving a gold medal in a Mustad fly-tying contest. He told me that he doesn't tie many featherwing flies these days; he's tied most of the patterns he wanted to try, and the cost of materials is getting prohibitive. Although he enjoys tying, he has never sold flies commercially.

Jim enjoys fishing for a variety of species. He and his wife fish the Stewiacke for stripers in the spring, and the Northumberland Strait rivers for browns. He has also fished in Labrador and the Great Lakes, and, judging by some of the impressive mounts in his fly-tying room, he is as good an angler as he is a fly tier. One of Jim's patterns, the McCoul Special, was featured in Paul Marriner's book, *Modern Atlantic Salmon Flies*. "I developed that fly as a modification of a West Coast steelhead pattern, the Comet, by adding some Krystal Flash," he says, adding that he uses head cement to coat the body of the fly to protect it from the fish's teeth. "I thought it would be a good fly for fall salmon fishing and it is. I caught nine salmon on one before I lost the fly."

McCoul Special

Tail:	Red hackle	Wing:	Orange Krystal Flash and
Body:	Silver Diamond Braid, built up to a cigar shape		orange calf tail

The Margaree Salmon Museum highlights Nova Scotia's sport-fishing history.

Margaree Salmon Museum

Sport fishing has a long and colourful history in Nova Scotia, and nowhere is that history more evident than at the Atlantic Salmon Museum in Margaree. Visitors come away with a renewed appreciation for the sport and the early anglers who practiced it.

The museum has a great assortment of early fishing equipment including rods, reels, lines and flies. The rod collection contains all the famous names: Payne, Leonard, Hardy, and so on. The well-known American rod maker H. S. "Pinky" Gillum was a regular visitor to the area and he donated several rods to the museum. On the Margaree he was considered as fine a fisherman as he was a rod maker, strong praise indeed. The reel collection ranges from massive Vom Hofes to beautiful reels from Hardy, Orvis, Leonard and J. W. Young, but my personal favourite is a reel made from the piston of a Model A Ford by a local angler, a testament to the ingenuity of early salmon fishermen.

Fly aficionados can spend an afternoon poring over the collection at the museum. Virtually every famous fly tier is represented: Lee Wulff, Poul Jorgensen, Dan Bailey, Megan Boyd , Wallace Doak and Joe Aucoin. The legendary Catskill fly-tying team of Harry and Elsie Darbee were long-time visitors to the Margaree and their work is also on display.

While the bulk of the museum's collection deals with sport fishing, the less savory aspects of life on the river are also represented. "Poachers' Corner" highlights the devious means developed over the years to take salmon from the river, from the spear and jig method to dynamite. An ancient flambeau, a wire basket in which birch bark was burned to allow salmon to be speared at night is also on display.

Paul Marriner

Paul is known to many Atlantic Canadian anglers and fly tiers through his writings in numerous books and magazine articles. He is associate editor and columnist for the *Canadian Fly Fisher*, the fly-tying columnist for *Eastern Woods & Waters*, and a regional editor of *Outdoor Canada* magazine. He has had several hundred articles published in major North American fly fishing and outdoor magazines, as well as in several foreign-language publications.

Born in Halifax in 1944, Paul went to Dalhousie University and the Technical University of Nova Scotia, graduating in mechanical engineering. He taught at the Royal Military College in Kingston, where he also received a master's degree. Later, he worked for the military, the Canadian Conservation Institute, and for over twenty years at Transport Canada, from which he retired in 1996.

Paul is an eight-time member of the Canadian team at the World and Commonwealth Fly Fishing championships, and he was the captain of the Canadian team from 1994 to 1996 and again in 2000. The P. M. Emerger is a creation of his that he used, with some success, during competition with the national team.

Paul fished as a boy growing up in Halifax, but didn't start fly fishing until he was twenty-one. He used to salmon fish when he came home on leave, and gradually he became interested in tying flies. He basically picked it up on his own through trial and error. He attended one formal course on tying featherwing salmon flies given by Jerome Molloy, but that was after he retired. Paul tied commercially for a while in Ontario, but now he ties for himself and for his books and articles.

Paul likes minimalist patterns that are simple to tie, but believes that form and function are important as well. "I don't want to spend six hours tying a fly, but it needs to have the motion and colour required to catch whichever fish you are after," he says.

Paul is the author of the very popular *Modern Atlantic Salmon Flies*, published in 2000. He also authored *How to Choose and Use Fly-tying Thread*, *Stillwater Fly Fishing: Tools and Tactics*, *Atlantic Salmon: A Fly Fishing Primer* (an Outdoor Writers award-winning book in 1994), *The Au Sable River Journal* and *The Miramichi River Journal*. In 1991 Paul won the Gregory Clark Award for outstanding contributions to the arts of fly fishing.

P. M. Hanging Emerger

Hook: Straight-eye barbless or debarbed nymph, numbers 10–18.
Thread: UNI 8/0, colour to suit.
Abdomen: Dubbed to imitate the nymph of the target species.
Hackle: Four turns. Colour to suit.

Thorax: Foam cylinder, black (or white, coloured to suit), diameter appropriate for hook size. Half-shank in length is a good guide but test is essential to confirm buoyancy and attitude.

A fly fisherman for more than thirty-five years, Paul has angled for Atlantic and Pacific salmon, trout, bass, and other fresh- and salt-water species in a dozen countries around the world. He organized the Commonwealth Fly Fishing Championships in 1993 at Nimpo Lake, BC. He has also made numerous appearances as a lecturer on fly fishing and fly tying.

Presently, Paul is working on another book with co-editor Robert Jones, a compendium of fly patterns from across Canada.

Nick Martinello

Nick was born in Sydney, Nova Scotia, in 1938 and grew up in Louisbourg with his mother while his father was overseas during World War Two. Nick later joined the military himself and served in the Canadian army for twenty-seven years before retiring to New Waterford on Cape Breton Island.

Nick fished as a boy growing up in Louisbourg and began fly fishing when he was thirteen. "A neighbour gave me an old Heddon bamboo rod with a King Eider line and an Alcock reel," recalls Nick. "I really enjoyed it and pretty soon almost all my fishing was with the fly rod. I gave away all my spinning gear except for one rod that I use for fishing mackerel in the summer."

Nick used to buy his flies from local stores, like Rudderham's in Sydney. He didn't begin fly tying until he was posted to Germany in the mid 1960s. He bought a Veniards fly-tying vice, the Old Salmo model, and starting tying flies. He never took a course, learning instead by taking flies apart and seeing how they were put together.

He found Sam Slaymaker's book *Tie a Fly, Catch a Trout* very helpful when he was starting out, but it was Poul Jorgensen's book on salmon flies that started him tying flies for salmon, and he still uses it today. He now has an impressive collection of angling and fly-tying books.

Nick retired from the military in 1983 and began tying commercially in 1985 for George Morris in Sydney, along with Albert Jenkins and Rick MacDonald. He

Super Shrimp

Hook:	Salmon 2/0 to 6 single or double
Antennae:	Red bucktail and red Krystal Flash
Tag:	Gold tinsel
First half of Body:	Orange ice chenille
Back (from the centre of the hook):	Golden pheasant tippet dyed red, golden pheasant body feather tied flat top and bottom
Second half of Body:	Red wool, ribbed with oval gold tinsel
Back (at the head of the hook):	Golden pheasant body feather tied flat top and bottom
Head:	Red

also worked in George's fly shop. He still ties commercially today, mostly custom orders or for friends.

When he was based in New Brunswick, Nick was able to meet some of the New Brunswick fly tiers and become familiar with their flies. "Once when I was on leave I brought down some Black Bear Green Butt flies that Frank Wilson had shown me and took them to Grand River," says Nick. "Frank used to run a fly shop up on the Nashwack. I was having good luck with them and everyone wanted to know what I was using." Nick is also partial to Newfoundland patterns as well as the Newfoundland tying style: "I like the moosehair wing and often tie patterns such as the Undertaker with a moosehair wing."

Nick likes a durable, sparsely-dressed fly, and he believes that confidence in your fly is an important part of successful fly fishing. He taught fly tying when he was based in Greenwood, Nova Scotia, mostly to the children of people in the Forces. He ties traditional featherwing salmon flies to donate to local fishing groups or for gifts. These days Nick is having fun experimenting with shrimp patterns for Atlantic salmon. He has a pattern he calls the Super Shrimp that he has had great luck in the fall on the Margaree. Nick fishes mostly on Cape Breton Island these days, including the Margaree, Middle and North rivers. He does some fishing for trout and has a preference for traditional soft-hackle English wet flies, but he also likes to use streamers. The Muddler and Mickey Finn are good, and he is a big fan of the Thunder Creek series of streamers.

Harris Miller

Harris was born in Halifax in 1921. Throughout an illustrious career as a soldier, medical doctor and Deputy Minister of Health for Nova Scotia, he always found time to participate in his love of fly tying, fishing for Atlantic salmon and competitive shooting. He fished as a boy and again when he was stationed in New-foundland during the war. "I started tying flies about thirty years ago when I took a course from Heck Wallis," he says. "I really enjoyed it and ended up teaching fly tying for the Halifax Rec-reation Department for twenty-five years." Many Nova Scotia fly tiers in the Halifax area credit Harris with introducing them to fly tying.

There are framed collections of Harris's salmon flies at the St. Mary's River Museum. He is obviously a master at tying traditional featherwings as well as hairwing flies. He took a course from Ron Alcott on tying the featherwings, and although he enjoys tying them, his favourite salmon flies are the Cosseboom and the Ross Special.

Harris emphasizes the importance of proportion in tying a fly, and feels that presentation of the fly is as critical as the pattern in many cases.

Harris has not developed any fly patterns of his own. He has modified a few, but he was content tying the existing patterns, and always taught his students to tie true to pattern.

Problems with cataracts have curtailed his fly tying in recent years, but Harris continues his interest in issues related to sport fishing in Nova Scotia. Over the years he has made significant contributions to sport fish conservation in the province; he was one of the founding members of the Nova Scotia Salmon Association and continues to actively participate in their work. In 2004 he served as patron for their scholarship committee. For many years Harris maintained a camp on Nova Scotia's Moser River.

Brian Osgood

Nova Scotia anglers will be familiar with Brian as the resident fly tier at Fishing Fever on Agricola Street in Halifax, where he has worked for the past eight years. Brian was born in Halifax in 1961, began fishing for brook trout when he was four years old, and was fly fishing by the time he reached ten. Brian's fly-tying career began when he received a fly-tying kit from his parents. He taught himself how to tie using the instruction booklet included with the kit and was soon turning out flies that caught fish. He later took a fly-tying class taught by Dave Larkin. He also attended two of Ron Alcott's workshops on tying traditional featherwing flies for Atlantic salmon. Although Brian seldom ties featherwing flies today, he believes that tying the tags, butts and bodies of these flies provided good training for all forms of fly tying.

Brian has been tying commercially for the past ten years. He likes to tie his flies almost low water and quite sparse. He is also partial to small flies and seldom ties flies in larger sizes—a #6 is a big fly for him. Brian attributes his preference for smaller flies to his early salmon fishing experiences on the Gold and La Have rivers on Nova Scotia's South Shore; low water meant that most of the time he was fishing small flies. All rules, however, are made to be broken, and Brian stresses that the time of year and water conditions have to be taken into consideration when selecting flies. For fall fishing, his favourite fly is usually a General Practitioner tied on a double hook. The Green Highlander is his favourite wet fly for salmon, and he likes the bomber as a dry fly. He is also partial to the Green Machine, which is not surprising as it caught his largest salmon to date, a twenty-pounder on the La Have in 1993. He prefers to tie it on a small double and fishes it wet.

Brian ties his bombers on Mustad 9672 hooks since his favourite hook, the 38941, is no longer available. Bombers are an exception to his love of small flies—he ties them on #2 hooks and says, he would tie them bigger if he could get a bigger hook.

For trout, he likes a fully dressed Grey Ghost. He ties it on Carrie Stevens hooks for trolling and on Mustad 3665A hooks for casting. In terms of dry flies, Brian favours the Adams. "It looks like everything and nothing. You can't beat it," he says.

Brian ties thousands of flies a year, but never finds it monotonous; he likes working with his hands, and he still finds it very relaxing.

Jack Ripley

Jack was born in 1935 in Amherst. He grew up there and served as a police officer with the Amherst Police Department for thirty-five years. Jack is well known in Nova Scotia through his tackle shop, Rip Tide Tackle, which he runs in Amherst. As a boy he bait fished for trout, often walking out of town to fish local brooks. He didn't start fly fishing until he was twenty-five years old.

His first attempts at tying his own flies came in 1955. "I bought a Thompson fly-tying vice from the Herters catalogue. I started out using sewing thread and some Eagle Claw bait hooks. Back then everyone used a three-fly cast with a nymph, wet fly and dry so I used to tie them." Later Jack would use Herters's own hooks. "They were called Black Pool hooks and were made by Reddich. They were a great hook and I still have a few that I use every now and then."

Jack turned to Joe Bates's *Atlantic Salmon Flies and Fishing* when he started tying. "That book ruined me for trout fishing," he laughs. "I really became interested in fly fishing for salmon and in tying salmon flies." While Jack has great admiration for traditional salmon flies and the people who tie them, he doesn't tie them himself. "I love the look of a Jock Scott or Green Highlander, but I don't want to spend an hour finishing the head of my flies." His love of traditional patterns extends to the use of jungle cock in his salmon flies, and he believes that a fly with jungle cock cheeks will out-fish one without it about three to one.

Jack's passion for tying flies led him to raise his own bantam roosters for hackle. He also raised a few pheasants.

While Jack tied flies commercially for many years and continues to tie custom orders, he gets his greatest enjoyment these days from tying flies for his own use. He loves the look of the Partridge Bartleet hook but most of the time uses the Mustad 36890 for his salmon flies. "It is a plain, simple hook that is not too expensive," he says. "I like a hook with a limerick bend; it gives a good solid hold."

Most of Jack's flies are small: "The majority of my flies are in the #6 to 10 size range. A #2 hook would be a big hook for me." He also has a preference for wet flies. "Old habits are hard to break," he says. "I like fishing flies down and across and have never had much luck with the dry fly for salmon."

Northeast Smelt

Tag:	Flat silver tinsel and Chinese red Uni-Stretch	Hook:	Mustad 3665A
Tail:	White polar bear over which is an equal amount of olive Fly Fur	Wing:	White goat topped by olive Fly Fur, no longer than the tail
Body:	Flat silver braided tinsel, two layers	Sides:	Matched olive grizzly saddle hackle enclosing wing
Hackle:	Red hackle fibres tied as a throat	Cheeks:	Jungle cock, slightly shorter than throat

Jack pays a lot of attention to how his flies are presented to the fish, generally using floating lines combined with sinking leaders of varying weights, depending on water conditions, to ensure the fly is swung at what he considers to be the proper depth.

Jack has had something to do with the recent popularity of the Lester the Lobster fly in Eastern Canada. "Brian Gairns brought the fly over from Prince Edward Island and asked me to tie him up a few," recalls Jack. "I was skeptical at first but soon found out how effective it is. I still tie it, mostly on Mustad 9672 hooks, as well as a pink version that I believe is just as good. I tied some for some anglers who were heading to Labrador. They cleaned up on Arctic char using Lester the Lobster."

Jack believes that he can tie six flies, all the same pattern, and pick one out that has a "certain something" that will make it fish better than the others. "I don't like a fly that is too sparse, but too much material is not good either," he says. "If you tie on a wing and think that it looks good then you probably have too much material—take some off." Jack is also a firm believer in building a sturdy fly: "I use cement on the body and throughout the process. Try to keep things neat and flat. Don't use too many wraps of thread and try to avoid making things too bulky."

Jack's flies appeared in Paul Marriner's *Modern Atlantic Salmon Flies*. "I tie a smelt imitation, the Northeast Smelt, which has been very successful for me on both trout and salmon, and my son Danny developed a pattern, the Highland Ghost, which is also a great fly for salmon."

Howard Ross

Howard was born in Sydney, Nova Scotia, in 1943. He now lives in New Glasgow, where he retired from a career as a pharmacist—or, as Howard describes it, a career as a salmon fisherman with time out to work as a pharmacist: "For years I scheduled my life and work around salmon fishing. If I didn't catch fifty salmon a year I considered it a poor season." Howard comes by his love of salmon fishing honestly. Growing up in Cape Breton, he was taught fly tying by Joe Aucoin and caught his first salmon under the guidance of famed St. Mary's River guide Dan MacIntosh.

Howard's father, Nip Ross, fished salmon and knew Joe Aucoin. Nip wanted Howard to learn to tie flies so that he could keep Nip supplied with them. He would drive Howard out to Joe Aucoin's home in New Waterford for lessons. Aucoin was "a quiet, patient man and it wasn't too long before I could tie a half decent salmon fly," says Howard. "The first fly he taught me to tie was a Cosseboom. Joe used to give me materials that he had left over from his commercial business. I would come home with capes and jungle cock necks with all the feathers and nails picked out of the centre; only the really big, or small stuff along the edge would be left."

Howard continued tying flies and soon began selling them at the Sports Mart in Sydney.

The St. Mary's River Interpretation Centre profiles the natural history and sport-fishing heritage of the region.

Memories of the St. Mary's River

Recently the St. Mary's River Association was able to build a new Visitor Centre and Museum on the banks of the river. It is located alongside Highway 7 at the picnic park just outside Sherbrooke. The beautiful new centre replaces the small green cabin that served as the association's headquarters for many years. The museum is open from June 1 until October 15 from 9:30 A.M. until 5:30 P.M. The main room of the centre serves as a museum which highlights the history of sport fishing on the St. Mary's as well as the natural history of trout and salmon. If you enjoy looking at old fishing rods and reels as well as reading about the fishing exploits of early anglers, you will certainly enjoy a trip to the centre, which also boasts a very knowledgeable staff who can answer your questions on both the river and the local area. The centre hosts a gift shop and meeting area.

Ross Special

Tag:	Silver oval tinsel	Wing:	Red squirrel tail
Tail:	Golden pheasant crest	Throat:	Yellow hackle tied as a
Body:	Red wool		collar and pulled down
Rib:	Oval silver tinsel	Cheeks:	Jungle cock (optional)

The story of his first salmon is a classic: "I was fishing with my father and grandfather at the Ford Pool on the St. Mary's. It was a bright, sunny day, so everyone else was up on the bench. I was just a young fellow and didn't know any better, so I was down on the pool flailing away. The first thing I knew I raised a fish, but I was excited, and pulled the fly away. I ended up raising, pulling the fly away from that fish, three times. My father and grandfather were hollering at me to hook the fish. Dan MacIntosh, who was sitting with them, came down and told me to take in my line. He checked my knot holding the fly and looked at the leader. Then he told me, 'Throw the same length of line out, take your hand off the reel and close your eyes.' I looked at him but did as he said, making a cast to the same spot in the pool and took my hand off the reel. 'Close your eyes,' he told me and the next thing I knew the fish was on and I was playing it."

Howard landed the fish, his first salmon.

Howard speaks highly of MacIntosh: "He was the complete package," he says. "He was a legend on the river, but he was the real deal; he knew every rock in that river, and he caught a lot of fish."

Howard's father also had a lasting impact on fly tying in Atlantic Canada, as the creator of the Ross Special. Howard explains: "My father came home and told my mother he asked Joe Aucoin to tie up a fly with certain colours, and that Aucoin had christened it the Ross Special." Of all Joe Aucoin's flies, the Ross Special is one of the most popular in Atlantic Canada today, especially for fall fishing.

As a very experienced and keen angler, Howard knows what makes a taking fly: "It has to have that look," he says. "It's the sort of thing that's hard to describe but you know it when you see it. I might tie ten flies and I will look at one of them and say, that's the one."

Howard is firmly believes that presentation is more important than the fly pattern. "You have to put it over them the right way. For many years I caught probably half my fish on the St. Mary's with one fly, the Pink Lady MacIntosh. For me, that was the fly and I fished it with a lot of confidence because I knew that I would catch salmon with it."

Larry Shortt

Larry was born in 1947 in Dartmouth and grew up in a fishing household; both his mother and father were avid anglers. Larry served in the air force for ten years before joining the Dartmouth Police Department, then later the Halifax Regional Po-

Bow River Bugger

Tail:	Olive marabou	Head:	Deerhair collar and gold,
Body:	Dark green Ice Chenille		silver or black cone head
Hackle:	Grizzly palmered through body		

lice Force, before retiring in 2001. He took up fly fishing in 1981 and it wasn't long before he discovered fly tying as well. "I took a course through the May Fly Tackle shop in 1983. Fred Harrigan, Clyde Paul and Reg Smith were involved with it at that time and I really took to it. I was never an artistic person but in fly tying I found something that I could do that allowed me to create something."

Larry found Stewart and Allen's book on Atlantic salmon flies very helpful, along with books by Jorgensen and Bates. He also found a television show by Warren Duncan (from Saint John, New Brunswick) on Maine Public Television to be an aid to his tying.

Larry's fly tying is a reflection of his love of fly fishing. "I love fishing for trout and salmon but I also fly fish for small-mouth bass and shad. Tying flies for those species is a lot of fun as well," he says. Larry's shad flies are the some of the neatest available, and his innovation has been recognized by authority and author Boyd Pfeiffer, who included Larry's shad patterns in the revised edition of *Shad Fishing*.

Larry ties his shad flies on Mustad 3366 flies, which have a straight eye. He gets his flies very shiny by using three coats of head cement. "The most important thing for a fly is that it catches fish," laughs Larry, "but to do that I feel that it should be neat with the proper proportions—not too big a head and not overly dressed." In keeping with Larry's fish-catching requirements, one of his favourite patterns is the Bow River Bugger. "I caught bass, rainbow, brook and brown trout on this pattern, as well as salmon. It is as close to an all-round fly as you will find. I tie it in a variety of colours."

Larry actively gives back to the sport he feels has given him so much over the years. He is a member of the Sackville Rivers Association as well as the Nova Scotia Salmon Association. He is also involved in the Sackville Rivers Association's fly-tying program, Flies and Lies. "We meet during the winter and have a lot of laughs; we even tie a few flies," jokes Larry.

Bill Strople

1944–2000

Bill was born in Antigonish County, Nova Scotia, and lived most of his life near his beloved St. Mary's River. He was a fixture at Silvers Pool, where he fished his much-loved White Muddler fly. He was one of the founding members of the St. Mary's River Association and served as president and treasurer of the organization. In

recognition of his work, he received an award for dedication to the association at its annual meeting in 1988.

His article "If I Only Had One Fly," from the April 1988 issue of the St. Mary's River Association News, details his experiences with his favourite fly:

Having spent most of the time living in the St. Mary's River area of Guysborough County, I have been fortunate in being able to experience the excellent Atlantic salmon and trout fishing which this area has to offer.

After having tied many different patterns of flies and experimenting with them on salmon and trout, there is only one fly which seems to have the edge over all the others—the Muddler Minnow. My first attempts at tying the Muddler were very crude, but they caught trout. Since then I have tied it in a wide range of sizes, dressed heavily to float or lightly to sink.

In 1978 I met an angler on a river system in Guysborough County named Charlie Woollie from New Glasgow. We met many times on the same system and eventually became good friends. One day he gave me a fly which he called the White Muddler, tied on a size 6 hook, 4X long. Every spring he ordered four dozen from Dan Bailey's Fly Shop in Livingston, Montana. The pattern seemed to work better on trout than the original Muddler Minnow. I began tying the fly in sizes 16 through 4/0. In smaller sizes, fished slowly, it imitates a nymph very well. In larger sizes, fished dry, it can also represent a floating insect.

The White Muddler has caught native speckled and sea-run trout, rainbow trout, brown trout, Atlantic salmon, striped bass and mackerel for me over the years. A few years ago striped bass were in great numbers in the Antigonish area. At that time I tied the White Muddler on a size 4/0 Mustad 94840 hook. The fly was tied to float high on the water yet when pulled it would pop under the water surface very quickly, leaving bubbles. Striped bass took the fly so well that I recall getting my knuckles rapped by the reel handle on a surprise strike.

During the winter of 1986 I was dreaming of how Atlantic salmon take the dry fly, and thoughts went back to the White Muddler I had designed for striped bass. So, over the winter months I tied this style in sizes from 8 through 3/0.

The 1986 season was one of the finest I have experienced. In June of that year large salmon were plentiful. I would float the Muddler over the salmon lie and the salmon would rise and take the floating Muddler very hard, leaving a hole in the

White Muddler

Hook:	4/0-16, 3X to 4X long shank, Limerick, Sproat or model Perfect style hook	Body:	White chenille, or wool for small sizes
Thread:	Black or red	Wing:	White turkey wing over white calf tail
Tag:	Silver wire	Shoulder:	Natural grey deer body hair, heavy to float, lightly dressed to sink
Tail:	White turkey wing, long as hook gap		
Butt:	Fluorescent salmon red chenille, or floss or wool	Head:	White deerhair trimmed to bullet shape
Rib:	Oval silver tinsel		

surface after they went down with the fly. In the month of June alone, I had caught and released fifteen large salmon in the 15-25 lb. class. For the rest of the season I used smaller versions of the White Muddler, which also worked quite well.

Since then I have given White Muddlers to some of my friends and they have done quite well with them in the fall on the West River, Antigonish and the East River, Pictou for Atlantic salmon. Also, during the past few years the New Brunswick deerhair patterns like the Buck Bug and Bomber have become quite popular in the St. Mary's area.

I believe the Muddler rates right up there with the other deerhair creations, so my fly boxes are full of dark and white Muddlers, tied both as wet and dry flies in sizes from 16 through 4/0. And, as I await another fishing season, I am busy tying Muddlers, like so.

Brian Sweeney

Brian was born in Halifax in 1964 and lives there today. He grew up fishing for trout with his father, and began fly fishing when he was eight or nine years old. A gift of a fly-tying kit soon had him tying flies as well. He is mostly self-taught, but he received lessons and advice from Eric Jefferson. He was another fan of Warren Duncan's fly-tying show on Maine Public Television: "The show ran for eight or ten weeks," recalls Brian, "and I watched every episode." Later he also attended workshops offered by Warren Duncan and Ron Alcott.

Brian credits several publications as being helpful to him as a fly tier. "Perhaps the most useful was Doak's catalogue," says Brian. "I used to study all the patterns in it." Poul Jorgenson's books and Dick Stewart and Farrow Allen's book on Atlantic salmon flies were also helpful.

Brian began tying flies commercially about twenty years ago. He is familiar to many anglers as the resident fly tier in Mike's Tackle Shop, which Mike Crosby ran on Agricola Street in Halifax. Brian worked in the store for ten years and stayed on for another year when it was sold to new owners, who renamed it Fishing Fever. Today Brian works as a fisheries technician with the Department of Fisheries and Oceans in Halifax, so his fly-tying time is limited; however, he continues

"Each river has its own character which is determined by the geophysical features of its watershed and the timing of the salmon's return. I was amazed and thrilled by the ruggedness of North River, awed by the tremendous pools of the Indian Brook, and charmed by the dainty features of the Clyburn Brook. Each of the others left a different but indelible impression."

James T. Grey,
Salmon Rivers of Cape Breton Island
(1984)

Surface Stonefly

Parachute Post: Yellow seed bead on bent pin	Body: Lime green floss, lacquered
Tag: Flat silver tinsel	Hackle: Grizzly
Wing: Black squirrel	

to tie for some clients, mainly fishing lodges in Quebec and Newfoundland and Labrador, as well as Fishing Fever.

Brian's specialty is flies for Atlantic salmon. "I haven't tied a trout fly commercially for years," says Brian. He ties mostly what the lodges want; they usually send him a selection of the flies they want—usually popular patterns that work on local rivers—and he copies them. "On the Gaspé they like flies in various combinations of green and black," he says, "while in Labrador they like small black flies such as the Blue Charm and Thunder and Lightning." Hook types also vary from region to region. Brian says that about sixty percent of his salmon flies are tied on traditional black japanned salmon hooks, with the remainder tied on bronze down eye hooks. "Doubles are also popular in Quebec," Brian says, "but I don't tie them for many other areas."

Brian stresses that a good fly begins with "a good vice, scissors and bobbins," he stresses. He ties on a Regal vice.

Brian likes to tie his flies fairly sparsely and believes that durability and proportions are important: "I have a fly that Eric Jefferson tied for me, a Brown Bug, that I caught thirty-two salmon on. I have it in a pocket of my vest and use it every year." If he had to pick one fly for salmon, it would be a Brown Bug with a green butt and brown hackle. He fishes it wet or dry and ties it on a #4 Mustad 3906 hook.

Brian's flies are featured in Paul Marriner's *Modern Atlantic Salmon Flies*. He has also taught several fly-tying classes, both at the store where he worked and through the Halifax school board continuing education program.

He enjoyed teaching, "especially when the class was interested in what I was teaching," he recalls. "I often felt that I learned as much as I taught, especially from the kids. They often approached tying problems in different, and often simpler ways than I would teach."

Neil Watson

Neil was born in Quincy, Massachusetts, in 1928 but moved to Nova Scotia with his parents as a young boy, first to Musquodoboit and then to Six Mile Brook in Pictou County. Later he moved to Westville, where he and his wife raised their family and Neil made his living as a carpenter—or, as he describes it, a jack of all trades. Neil began fishing as a small boy in Six Mile Brook and his love of the sport continues to this day.

Neil is a master fly tier; he's been tying flies for over forty years and has been instrumental in teaching fly tying to many young anglers in the local area. He began tying flies when he was twenty-six. He watched William MacLean, a local fly tier, and picked up the craft. Neil first tied trout flies, mainly British patterns such as the Cow Dung or King and Queen of the Waters. He began tying salmon flies after he started salmon fishing about thirty-five years ago; he was going through so many salmon flies that he had to start tying his own. He tied the Green Highlander, Ross Special, Cosseboom, and MacIntosh—all popular flies at that time.

Neil warns against dressing flies too heavily, and adds that "if you don't put it over the fish correctly then it doesn't make any difference which pattern you use. I often have people ask me for a dozen flies that will catch salmon. I always tell them that I can tie them flies that I can catch salmon with, but I can't guarantee that they will catch fish with them."

The Green Machine tied on a #4 bronze down eye hook is without question Neil's favourite salmon fly. He ties it with green wool instead of deerhair since he always fishes it wet. "I find that the colour of the butt is also important. I add the green butt first and then the orange…For some reason, if I only add a green butt I mostly hook grilse." He is a big fan of dry fly fishing for Atlantic salmon. "When the water warms up…I find a green bomber with a yellow or white calftail wing and tail to be very effective. Last year I had some chestnut brown deerhair that I used for some bugs and bombers. I tied it with white calftail at the tail and wing. For some reason that fly was great at locating fish. I didn't hook many on it but I often hooked them on another fly later."

Neil usually ties on bronze down eye Mustad hooks. "I often open up the gape with pliers," he says. "It makes it easier to hook fish." Neil also pinches the barb on all his salmon flies to aid in release. "I usually give a fish slack line after a couple of jumps and many times—not always—they will release themselves." If someone requests them, Neil will tie his salmon flies on Mustad 36890 hooks. "I find them too dull, so I touch them up with the file before I tie with them. I also tell people to touch them up when they are fishing with them on the river—a rock will do in a pinch. You need a sharp hook—it will penetrate better."

Three of Neil's patterns—the East River Special, Watson's Green Machine and the St. Mary's River Special—are featured in Paul Marriner's *Modern Atlantic Salmon Flies*. Neil is constantly experimenting with either new patterns or different ways of tying existing ones. "Take the Ross Special, for example," he tells me. "Although it is a great fall fly on its own, I added a golden pheasant crest and an orange butt and found that it fished much better than the original." Neil also offers a clever tip: "When I come up with a new pattern I always tie two of them. I'll fish with one, and if I have some luck

Neil's Green Machine

Tail:	Red phentex	Body:	Green wool
Tag:	Green wool then orange wool	Hackle:	Brown palmered over the body

with it and happen to lose it—hopefully in a big fish—I'll have another one home that I can use as a pattern instead of trying to remember how I tied it."

Neil is disappointed in the decline of Atlantic salmon. He remembers fishing the Stewiacke River one morning in 1983 when 109 salmon were caught. He also remembers the glory days on the St. Mary's, where he caught his best fish to date, a twenty-six-pounder. He feels the decline is due to a combination of factors, like poaching and habitat loss. These days, he is content to practice hook-and-release when salmon fishing. He is also active in conservation work, and he was one of the founding members of the Pictou County Rivers Association. Neil is also an avid trout angler and he feels that trout stocks have fared a little better than salmon. He and his wife get out every spring for some trout fishing.

Neil has several favourite trout flies, but if he had to pick one it would be a woolly worm tied with an orange body.

Although he has battled illness in recent years, Neil continues to tie every day. Last winter he tied a collection of salmon wet flies that his son framed for him. It is a beautiful collection of the work of a master fly tier. He continues to hunt, bagging an eight-point buck last fall: "I saved the hide for flies," he confides.

He favours hen hackle for his wet flies, saying that it is softer and has better movement in the water. "You need good stiff hackle for your dry flies though," he says.

Damian Welsh

Damian credits his grandfather, Lee Bushell, for his interest in fly tying: "My grandfather started tying his own flies for his own fishing and I loved watching him as he spun feathers and thread onto a hook at the kitchen table," recalls Damian. "It wasn't long before he allowed me to use his vice and materials whenever we visited. The only patterns he tied were small streamers of his own creation. I still have dozens of his flies that I take out every now and then to admire."

Damian was born in Antigonish, Nova Scotia, in 1975, and his interest in fly tying soon prompted him to purchase his own equipment and begin to tie flies. He bought his first vice, a Sunrise AA, and a few tools and supplies when he was around twelve years old.

Damian's interest grew over the years and eventually led him to begin tying flies commercially through a small fly shop he opened at his home, the South River Fly Shop. As his experience grew, he began tying different patterns and experimenting with different techniques and materials. "My interest in salmon flies

Mickey Finn

Body:	Silver tinsel		bucktail then yellow buck-
Wing:	Yellow bucktail topped		tail
	with a small bunch of red	Cheeks:	Jungle cock

also led me to begin tying classic salmon flies. I see it as a natural progression for my fly tying as I take my tying to another level," he says.

Although Damian ties many patterns for his commercial business, his personal favourite continues to be a classic streamer pattern, the Mickey Finn. "I use the Mickey Finn as a searching pattern and it has been a consistent producer for me," recalls Damian.

Along with his grandfather, Damian credits several fly tiers with having a major influence on him and his fly tying: "I learned a lot from the writings of Lee Wulff, Poul Jorgensen, Dick Talleur, Michael Radencich, Rick Whorwood, Ronn Lucas and Monte Smith. Some other regional fly tiers who have influenced my fly tying are Jerry Doak, Warren Duncan, Jacques Heroux, Jerome Molloy and Bryant Freeman as well as many friends and fellow fly tiers on flytyingforum.com."

Damian likes to tie "pretty flies, flies that are pretty to the angler but also pretty to the fish. Proportions are also important but I also think you need some variety in your fly box. Having twelve identical flies of the same size and pattern is not as useful as having different sizes of that fly with some tied with a lot of material and some tied very sparse. That way you can change what you are offering to the fish depending on conditions on the water."

He ties on a variety of hooks and favours the Partridge CS42 for his Bombers, while using a Mustad 79580 for many of his streamers and the 94840 for his dry flies. Although the Mickey Finn is his favourite all-around fly, Len Rich's Big Intervale Blue is his favourite salmon pattern.

Damian runs his commercial fly-tying business, River's Edge Fly Fishing, from his home in Port Hawkesbury, and has recently founded the Nova Scotia Fly Tier's Association, a society dedicated to the preservation and teaching of fly tying in Nova Scotia. "I really wanted to preserve the history and educate people on fly tying in Nova Scotia," he says. "Hopefully I will be able to hold some fly-tying seminars and possibly a fly-tying show at some point in the future."

J. E. "Jamie" Webb

Jamie was born in Brantford, Ontario, in 1971 and moved with his family to Digby, Nova Scotia, when he was six months old. Later moves ensued as his father, an RCMP officer, was transferred throughout the Maritimes. Jamie moved to Truro, where he now lives, in 1992.

Jamie remembers fishing for bluefish off the wharf in Digby, where offal from the fish plant served as chum to bring fish into the wharf. His fly fishing began when he was living in Cardigan on Prince Edward Island. "It was around 1985 and I was bait fishing for trout," recalls Jamie. "I wasn't having any luck. Another angler who was fly fishing was catching fish so I decided that I wanted to learn how to do it." Jamie and his family lived close to the Cardigan Fish Hatchery, which stocked the Cardigan River with brook and rainbow trout, as he soon discovered.

His fly tying began a year later when he ordered some flies from a local tier who didn't deliver them on time. He decided that he would try to tie them himself, and he has been tying ever since.

With a small bait and tackle business run from his home, it wasn't long before Jamie was also selling flies commercially. Some friends who tied flies helped him in the beginning, and he also attended a course. Several books proved helpful when he started, including Dave Hughes's *American Fly Tying Manual*.

These days Jamie mostly ties custom orders for trout and salmon flies. A lot of his flies are bought by Nova Scotia anglers who are either fishing in the province or in Newfoundland and Labrador.

He ties most of his dry flies on Mustad 94840 hooks, while he prefers Partridge or Alec Jackson spey hooks for his salmon flies. Over the years Jamie has become interested in tying traditional featherwing Atlantic salmon flies, and he credits Ron Alcott's book *Building Classic Salmon Flies* as a big help to him. He sells presentation flies and also donates them to conservation groups.

Jamie likes to tie his fishing flies with correct proportions, especially his dry flies. "I also tie differently depending on condition," he says. "For example I tie my MacIntosh flies very sparse, with only a half-dozen hairs from a red squirrel tail for a wing and two turns of hackle, if the water is low. In higher water you need a more fully dressed fly."

Jamie believes in tying quality flies: "I wouldn't sell a fly to anyone that I wouldn't use myself," he says.

Jamie's favourite salmon fly is the Buck Bug, tied with deer or elk hair; he finds caribou hair too soft. He usually ties it with an orange butt and a natural brown body with an orange hackle palmered through it. "I caught my first salmon on the Morell River in Prince Edward Island on a deerhair fly, a Green Machine," recalls Jamie, "and they are still my favourites."

Jamie also enjoys fly fishing and tying flies for American shad, chain pickerel and small-mouth bass. For pickerel and bass, he likes top water flies and has had his best luck with Lefty's Deceivers tied with light blue and white bucktail. He says his favourite flies trout are his own Creation and the Upside Down Dun, tied with cul de canard feathers.

"At Yarmouth we encountered heavy fog and to me it was meeting an old friend from across the continent. Long before we ran into this lowering silver bank of fog I could smell it.… Here we disembarked and took a train, without being able to see what the port looked like. Some ten miles on we ran out of the fog into bright sunshine and I found the Province of Nova Scotia to be truly of the northland, green and verdant and wild, dotted with lakes and areas of huge grey rocks, and low black ranges covered with spruce, and rivers of dark clear water."

Zane Grey,
Tales of Swordfish and Tuna
(1927)

Chapter 5

Fly Tiers of Prince Edward Island

"If there's a Valhalla for brook trout fishermen it must look like Prince Edward Island....More than 20 streams run seaward in all directions along the periphery of this island province....While's there's excellent brook trout fishing along the thousands of miles of streams, this is really the domain of the salter. It's rated tops by the hordes of local anglers, and almost everyone on the island seems to be a trout fisher."

Nick Karas, Brook Trout *(1997)*

Nestled in the Gulf of St. Lawrence, "the Island" has been hailed as the Garden of the Gulf for its agricultural production. It is also a popular tourism destination, and it offers some of the best brook trout fishing in Atlantic Canada. Along its almost two thousand kilometres of coastline are numerous barrier beaches and food-rich estuaries where trout congregate to feed on bait fish, sand shrimp and other invertebrates. Trout enter saltwater during the late spring and return as well-fed sea-run trout that weigh from one to five pounds.

The Island's short spring-fed streams, which maintain good flows of cool water during the summer months, also benefit trout; other Atlantic Canadian rivers can suffer from low and warm water conditions that force trout into small feeder streams. While brook trout are the most popular and common species on the Island, rainbow trout are stocked in Glenfinnan and O'Keefe's lakes and are found in a few streams.

Although less well known for its Atlantic salmon–angling opportunities, Prince Edward Island has five main rivers that support salmon. The Morell is perhaps the best known, but the Valleyfield, Dunk, West and Trout rivers also have runs of salmon. Most of the salmon runs are composed of grilse, supported by hatchery stocking from the Cardigan Fish Hatchery, but there are also larger multi-sea winter salmon caught every season.

As in the other Atlantic Canadian provinces, trout and salmon are the main species targeted by Prince Edward Island anglers. However, fly fishing opportunities also exist on the Island for white perch and Atlantic mackerel. All this on an island which, in addition to being the smallest province in Canada, is also the most densely populated.

The innovation and variety of patterns developed on the Island are impressive. Over the years local anglers have crafted patterns such as the Blockhouse and Orange Shrimp for sea run-trout; recently they have modified and created shrimp patterns such as Lester the Lobster for both trout and salmon. The number of patterns developed for Atlantic salmon is especially interesting, with materials ranging from seal fur to dryer lint.

Eric Arsenault

Eric was born in Charlottetown in 1946 and lived there until he was eighteen. At that time he joined the Royal Bank and was transferred to Windsor, Ontario. He spent five years at the bank and returned home to work with Canadian National Railways. Eric joined Parks Canada in 1986, and he remained with them until he retired. Eric began fishing as a young boy, and used to ride his bike to the outskirts of town to fish. He became interested in fly fishing after seeing another boy catching trout with flies after Eric had gone fishless using worms. His father advised him against fly fishing, telling Eric: "It's hard to do and you'll lose too many flies in the trees." Eric persevered, however, and purchased a fly-fishing outfit with money raised from his paper route: "I purchased it at the Bike Shop in Charlottetown, the only store selling fly-fishing equipment at that time. The flies all came from Alcocks in England," he says.

Eric began fly tying after suffering a car accident when he was sixteen years old. He ended up in the hospital with ninety-six stitches in his leg. The patient in the bed next to him was Joe Hennessey, who ran a shoe repair business in Charlottetown. Luckily for Eric, Hennessey was also an avid angler and fly tier, and after both were out of the hospital, he taught Eric how to tie flies. When Eric became proficient, Hennessey suggested he visit Frank Longaphie, a professional fly tier in Charlottetown who sold his flies under the brand name of Old Master Brand. Eric began hanging around the shop and eventually Frank asked him to help out. "Frank taught me a lot about fly-tying materials," recalls Eric. One of the old-time patterns that Eric continues to tie from the old days is the Blockhouse fly, developed for fishing sea trout off the

Eric's Bug

Body:	Carved balsa wood painted black and dubbing	Hackle:	Palmered over body

Blockhouse in Charlottetown. It continues to be a popular fly pattern today.

Later Eric met Jack Gay, an avid angler and fly tier. Gay taught Eric a lot about fly tying but also taught him how to build and repair fishing rods.

Eric began tying flies commercially while working for the Royal Bank in Ontario. "I was hired to tie flies for all the Stedman stores in Northern Ontario and tied about ten thousand flies for them. Eventually, however, I found that the commercial tying took too much time away from my family and fishing, so I decided to stop," he says.

When Eric returned to the Island, he began tying some flies for Mike Fitzgerald and Stu Simpson, who were in business at that time. A flexible fly tier who believes any fly will catch fish under the right conditions, Eric ties his commercial flies by the book. "I tie what the customer wants," he says. "I tie mostly trout flies and I get a great deal of enjoyment from developing flies to match local conditions."

One of Eric's innovative patterns is a fly he calls Eric's Bug, which imitates a variety of emerging insects. "It floats very well and I have caught both trout and salmon with it," Eric says. "The body consists of the balsa wood, which is attached to the hook by inserting a length of monofilament through the wood and attaching it with Krazy Glue. The mono is attached to the hook with thread, then I add black dubbing and palmer a black hackle over the dubbing."

Now retired, Eric has more time for fishing and fly tying. During the winter he does custom fly tying for clients and teaches fly tying at community schools. When summer comes, Eric moves to Ben's Lake, outside of Charlottetown, where he works at the campground selling flies and doing some guiding. While Eric enjoys all types of fishing, his favourite continues to be fishing dry flies for native brook trout.

"All my fish are released and I use barbless hooks for my flies," Eric says. He is active in a number of sport-fishing organizations, including the Atlantic Salmon Federation, the Prince Edward Island Salmon Association, the Montague Watershed Enhancement Committee, and the Federation of Fly Fishers. Eric has an impressive collection of angling books, and he puts them to good use in both his own tying and as a reference source for local tiers. "I often get calls from tiers asking me about certain patterns. A fellow called me the other day asking how to tie a Purple Drummer. I enjoy being able to provide them with the information they need."

Harmen Boshuis

Harmen was born in Charlottetown in 1958 and grew up there. He left to work in the aerospace industry and worked in Quebec and Nova Scotia before returning to Charlottetown about fifteen years ago. Harmen began fishing as a boy, but he didn't begin fly fishing until his time in Sydney, when he was introduced to fly fishing for trout and enjoyed it. When he moved back to Prince Edward Island, he pursued his interest by taking a fly-fishing course offered through the community schools program. He took the

Damselfly Nymph—Olive Twist

Hook:	9671 size 12	Body:	Olive nymph rope
Thread:	Olive	Shell Back:	Peacock herl
Tail:	Olive micro chenille	Legs:	Olive rubber (fine)
	(twisted)	Eyes:	Extra small plastic eyes
Under Body:	Two brass beads (1/8)		

course for three years, and at the end of the third year his instructor asked him if he was interested in teaching it. Harmen taught for nine years.

Harmen began tying commercially about ten years ago and supplied trout flies to stores on the Island. In 2004, he bought out two Charlottetown fishing retailers and opened his own store, Going Fishing, in Charlottetown. One of the businesses purchased by Harmen was owned by Stu Simpson, and Harmen credits Stu for encouraging him to get into the business. Harmen continues to tie commercially and to teach fly-tying classes at the store; local tiers Lorne Kaiser and Dwayne Miller keep the store supplied with trout and salmon flies, respectively. Harmen has an excellent selection of flies in his shop, including a wall display of snelled trout flies. He says that there are some anglers who like to fish a two-fly rig and use the snelled flies as the bob or dropper. Some anglers who find it difficult to tie on flies due to poor eyesight or arthritis find it much easier to attach the snelled flies.

Harmen says the big sellers early in the spring for trout are big flies. "I was tying Woolly Worms on 8X shank hooks last spring. Woolly Worms, Leeches, Muddler Minnows—they are all popular early in the season."

More anglers on the Island are apparently fishing nymphs with a strike indicator. "I tie a Damselfly Nymph which I have had some luck with," says Harmen.

"Later in the season most people fish dry flies, and the Mosquito, Adams, Green Drake and Blue Dun are all popular patterns," Harmen continues. One pattern that is very popular for trout on the Island is the Butterfly. Although most anglers now fish it for salmon, it was originally designed as a trout fly. Harmen ties it in small sizes, #12–#14, as both a dry and wet fly. For his dries he uses calf tail or goat hair wings as in the original, but when he wants to fish it wet he uses duck or goose quill fibres for the wings; he finds it sinks better. Both his wet and dry styles use Krystal Flash for a tail, a tinsel tag, red or green butt and peacock herl for the body.

Salmon anglers on the Island have been having success with flies that are not often thought of as salmon flies—patterns such as Woolly Buggers in red, purple, brown and black are effective, as are leech patterns and Woolly Worms.

Harmen also ties for clients who fish in other areas, "mostly traditional patterns—Black Bears, Cosseboom, Blue Charm and so on. We do tie differently depending on where the anglers are fishing. Newfoundland flies tend to be sparse, while we tie flies for New Brunswick rivers a little fuller." As both a tier and a retailer, Harmen says that durability is critical to a fly.

Good materials are important for Harmen's commercial ties, and to ensure top quality he often dyes and bleaches his own materials. He credits Bryant Freeman of Escape Anglers in Riverview, New Brunswick, with helping him with this aspect of his tying. He is also a fan of Bryant's Medway hooks for his salmon flies.

Green Cross

Tag:	Oval silver tinsel	Rib:	Oval silver tinsel
Body:	Rear half, fluorescent green floss veiled by a strand of the same; front half, peacock herl	Wing:	Natural black squirrel tail
		Collar:	Black hackle

Tom Corcoran

Tom was born in 1948 in Lynn, Massachusetts, and first came to Prince Edward Island to play football for St. Dunstens College in Charlottetown. Tom was drafted by the American military in 1969 and served for two years before coming back to Prince Edward Island to finish his university degree. He continued his studies in psychology at the University of Maine in Orono before returning to the Island in 1977, and has served as a guidance counsellor in the provincial school system and at Holland College ever since.

Tom fished with his father as a boy and did some fishing when he was in university, but he only began fly tying after taking a course from Mike Fitzgerald in Charlottetown. Although Tom never tied commercially, he helped out at Fitzgerald's shop and ran it for a year.

Tom enjoys fishing with small flies and ties a lot of his flies on #12 hooks, often in a low-water style. Except for spring black salmon fishing, he seldom ties any fly larger than a #6. He caught his largest salmon to date on a #10 dry fly in the St. Mary's River in Nova Scotia.

Tom likes green and black flies for salmon fishing. His favourites are the Rodgers Fancy and one of his own flies, the Green Cross, which was featured in Farrow and Allen's book *Flies for Atlantic Salmon*.

Besides the courses he took from Mike Fitzgerald, Tom also attended Ron Alcott's fly-tying workshops when he came to Charlottetown. Gary Anderson's Atlantic salmon book is one of Tom's favourite references, and he also enjoyed reading Hugh Falkus's book on salmon fishing. Tom has an interest in the sport-fishing and fly-tying history of Prince Edward Island and has written about some of the early fly tiers. One of Tom's patterns, the Green Cross, is featured in Farrow and Allen's book, *Flies for Atlantic Salmon*.

Art Eldershaw

Art was born in Morell and has lived there all his life. After spending time in the armed forces, he returned home, where he worked with Babineau Fisheries for thirty-three years. Although he fished as a boy, Art first became interested in fly fishing and fly tying about forty years ago: "My foreman at the fish plant fly fished and he got me started fly fishing for trout," recalls Art. "I didn't salmon fish until the mid-1980s, when the hatchery in Cardigan began stocking salmon in the Morell river." Art has been an enthusiastic salmon angler ever since.

An old timer on the Morell, Elmer Livingstone, used to supply Art with flies. Eventually Livingstone decided it was time Art learned to tie for himself, so he taught him the basics. The first fly Art tied was a Dark Montreal.

Elmer provided Art with some materials and Art has been tying ever since. Although he never tied commercially, Art tied for his own use and to give away to friends. At one time he tied about five hundred a winter, but now he ties about 100 to 150, mostly salmon flies.

Art helped to popularize the Lester the Lobster salmon fly on the Island: "Arnett Ives was out in British Columbia and he brought back a fly which was popular out there, the Squamish Poacher. He asked me to tie some up for him so I did. The fly became very popular on the Morell and some anglers use it for sea trout as well. I'm not sure who came up with the 'Lester the Lobster' name."

Art says that black flies are popular for salmon on the Morell, and that many have luck with the Black Ghost butterfly.

Art ties most of his salmon flies on #8 Mustad 36890 hooks and likes a fully dressed fly. One of his favourite patterns, the ART, was featured in Stewart and Allen's book *Flies for Atlantic Salmon*. Art says that his grandson, seven at the time came up with it. "He picked out the different materials on my fly-tying desk and I put them on the fly," he laughs.

Art uses a variety of materials in his flies: "I've even used lint from the dryer as dubbing for trout flies," he recalls. "When you put floatant on it, it makes a great dry fly body." His favourite trout fly is the Female Mosquito tied on a #12 hook, with a red, yellow or green butt. Art taught fly tying for several years at community schools and enjoyed passing on what he knew to other tiers.

"When sea-trout are newly arrived they will rise, even on a bright day, at almost any description of fly.... Say that there has been a gradual falling of the water, and the fish are disposed to linger as they arrive in the pools from the main river, awaiting the advent of rain, careful fishing with a small 'Doctor' or 'Ranger' or 'Admiral,' in the early morning or towards the evening, is sure to be rewarded with success."

Arthur Silver,
Farm-Cottage,
Camp and Canoe in Maritime Canada
(1907)

Black Ghost Butterfly

Tail:	Yellow hackle	Wing:	White calf tail tied in and divided
Body:	Black floss		
Rib:	Oval silver tinsel	Throat:	Yellow hackle

Mike Fitzgerald

Mike was born in Alberton in 1947 and grew up in Charlottetown, where a neighbour introduced him to fly fishing for trout. An interest in fly tying soon followed, and he attended a course offered by Robert Dufour through a community schools program in Charlottetown. Mike credits a few other tiers as major influences on his fly tying, including local fly tier Brian Lewis: "Brian ran the sports department at a local store and I learned a lot from him. I also travelled over to New Brunswick to take fly-tying courses from Warren Duncan, Dave Whitlock and Ron Alcott."

Mike was soon tying commercially for various outlets: "I tied some flies for Jerry Doak in New Brunswick and for a few other stores. At that time Lorne Kaiser and Harold 'Tutty' MacKinnon were tying most of the flies sold in Charlottetown and I didn't want to compete with them."

In 1980, Mike opened a retail fishing business, Island Rod and Flies, out of his home in Bonshaw near the West River. At that time the air force base in Summerside was operating, and much of Mike's business came from anglers on the base who fished the West River. Local tiers like Art Eldershaw supplied him with flies and Tom Corcoran helped out in the shop. Mike also did some guiding on the West and Morell Rivers.

The popular patterns when Mike was selling flies were mostly trout flies; salmon fishing wasn't good in the area until after Mike had closed the business. Anglers were usually after brook trout, and saltwater fishing for sea trout was popular in the spring. Most anglers used traditional patterns such as the Red Ibis, Orange Shrimp or Mickey Finn. Later on, when the water warmed up, anglers switched to flies like the Dark Montreal, Wickham's Fancy and Black Gnat.

Mike believes that proportions and good materials are important in fly tying. His quest for materials has led him to an unusual activity: picking up road kill. "When I made a trip over to New Brunswick during the summer months, I would often come home with a road-kill groundhog in the trunk of the car. There are none on Prince Edward Island and I liked to use the guard hair for tails on my Royal Coachman flies," laughs Mike.

Mike believes that a snelled fly tied on a Mustad 3906B is a good choice for sea-run trout. He also like the Mustad 94840 for his dry flies.

While Mike was busy working full-time as a school teacher and running his fishing business, he also found time to work on sport-fishing habitat and conser-

Saltwater Shrimp

Body:	Orange chenille	Hackle:	Orange
Rib:	Oval silver tinsel		

vation projects on the Island: "We had a very active Federation of Fly Fishermen chapter and carried out fish habitat projects on the West River," he says.

Mike eventually sold his business to Stu Simpson and no longer ties commercially. He continues to be an active angler, however, making a trip to Labrador every year for salmon and frequent trips to New Brunswick for small-mouth bass. One of Mike's flies, the Polar Silver, was featured in Dick Stewart's and Farlow Allen's *Atlantic Salmon Flies*.

Dave Fram

Dave was born in Windsor, Nova Scotia, in 1940 and moved to Halifax when he was five. He attended Mount Allison, Acadia and Dalhousie Universities. He received his professional designation in real estate and ran his own business, Balmoral Real Estate, for twenty years. He later joined Canada Mortgage and Housing and transferred to Charlottetown in 1989, where he worked until his retirement in 1999.

Dave remembers fishing in Halifax Harbour and off Point Pleasant Park as a young boy for pollack, sculpin and cunners. He also fished trout in New Brunswick when he visited his uncle's farm in Petitcodiac. His fly fishing began when he met Clyde Morse and his three sons in Halifax, who had a fishing camp along the Eastern Shore of Nova Scotia and taught Dave how to fly fish for trout. Later they introduced him to salmon fishing in the Stewiacke River.

Dave's fly tying began with a course taught by Fred Harrigan at the May Fly tackle shop in Halifax. He enjoyed tying flies and would later teach fly tying for the Halifax Recreation Department. Dave was instrumental in bringing Ron Alcott up to Halifax and Charlottetown to teach classes on tying traditional featherwing salmon flies. Dave ties some classics and enjoys it very much.

Dave's interest in fly tying led him to learn more about early fly tiers, and the result is a very impressive collection of fly-fishing and fly-tying books. Dave wasn't content just to tie classic salmon flies; he also wanted to fish them. "Ron Alcott and I each tied a fully-dressed Green Highlander and went fishing in the Forks Pool on the Margaree River," recalls Dave. "Ron lost his in the pool and while I didn't catch any fish on that trip, I hooked and released a salmon in Labrador on that fly."

Dave is always on the lookout for new and innovative flies and fly-tying methods; his latest interest are spey flies. His interest developed from an experience he had at the Red Bank Pool on the Margaree: "I fished through the pool without

Silver Fox

Hook:	Partridge, Single Wilson 2 to 10, or Partridge M 2/0 to 8	Body:	Black floss crochet material; wool works as well
		Throat:	Grizzly hackle
Tag:	Fine oval silver tinsel, three turns	Wing:	Silver fox with well-defined black tips flowing to white
Ribbing:	Fine oval silver tinsel, five turns	Shoulder:	Jungle cock
Head:	Black		

moving a fish and was followed by two anglers who each hooked fish on spey flies and I have been a fan ever since."

Dave's favourite type of fishing is dry fly fishing for Atlantic salmon, and his favourite flies for the task are Smokey Ball's Bombers. "He ties the best bugs I have ever seen," says Dave. A second favourite is the Green Machine. Dave also enjoys trout fishing and favours small dry flies, such as the Elk Hair Caddis or small Wulffs. Dave and his wife Bertha have a camp on the Margaree and spend the summer and fall there.

Dave believes proportion is important when tying a fly and likes a fly to look right. "The wing should extend slightly past the bend and I like the fly body tapered in a cigar shape," he says. "Jungle cock eyes also add to the attraction of a fly and there should be five turns of rib."

Dave feels strongly that the skills he learned from Ron Alcott in tying traditional featherwing salmon flies have served him well in his regular tying. Ron Alcott also influenced Dave's choice of a fly-tying vice—an HMH, the same model Alcott uses. "I like the rotary feature," Dave commented. "It lets me look at the fly from every side."

Fishing is a big part of Dave's life and he credits salmon fishing with teaching him patience: "Spending time on the river, fishing and meeting with other anglers, has taught me the importance of taking the time to slow down. For me, the camaraderie of talking to other anglers, exchanging flies and talking about the fishing is a big part of the sport."

Dave was the founding president of the Prince Edward Island Salmon Association and is currently a director of the Margaree Salmon Association; he coordinates their Lake O'Law Habitat project with Trout Nova Scotia. When he lived in Nova Scotia he served on the board of directors of the Nova Scotia Salmon Association.

Dave developed the Silver Fox fly because he has a personal connection to the material: his grandfather once ran a silver fox farm in New Brunswick and Dave can remember seeing the then-empty cages and barns when he visited as a boy. Dave likes the silver fox wing because it's softer than other hair, and as a result has more movement in the water.

Jeanne Jenkins

Jeanne was born in 1964 in Toronto and moved to the Island when she was five years old. She fished as a girl, but her fly fishing and fly tying began when she was thirty. A friend introduced her to fly tying and she attended a community school fly-tying program taught by the late John Hayes of Montague: "I took to the fly tying immediately," says Jeanne, "and after the third class the men attending the course asked me to stop as I was progressing faster than the rest of the class." Since that time Jeanne has tied with many well-known fly tiers, such as Jerome Molloy and Ron Alcott.

Her talent for fly tying led Jeanne to become a commercial tier in 1996. Her business includes saltwater flies for mackerel—she tied fifty thousand last year—in addition to her trout and salmon fly business. Many of Jeanne's trout and salmon flies are custom orders for clients fishing throughout Atlantic Canada. She ties most of her salmon flies on the Medway hooks carried by Escape Anglers in Riverview, New Brunswick. Most of her trout flies are tied on standard Mustad bronze hooks.

Jeanne says that among her customers the Black Bear Green Butt is always popular for salmon fishing, and that on the Island a lot of people fish the estuaries for sea trout so the silver body Orange Shrimp is a big seller.

Jeanne believes a fly should be sparse, small headed, and well proportioned. She is in demand as a fly tier at shows like the Isaac Walton Fly Fishers show in Ontario and the Atlantic Sports and RV show in Halifax, and has taught fly tying for the Becoming an Outdoors Woman program on Prince Edward Island. She is also in the process of organizing a fly-tying club in a local school.

Jeanne has developed a couple of successful flies. "One is the Black Labrador. This is a very versatile pattern; if adapted and tied on smaller hooks for trout and on larger hooks for salmon, a simple shift in materials will change it from a wet to a dry fly. The second is Jeanne's Morell Butterfly, my own variation of the traditional butterfly pattern, which I tie from #16 to #6."

Lorne Kaiser

Lorne was born in Grand Tracadie, Prince Edward Island, in 1924. He moved with his family to York when his father bought a farm there, and to Charlottetown in 1945, where they operated a store. Lorne joined Christies as a salesman and remained with them for thirty-eight very successful years.

Lorne began fishing when the family moved to Charlottetown. A friend, George Carson, introduced him to fly fishing. Lorne remembers taking his wife and family out fishing for the day. They would fish the tide for sea trout, a common activity for families at that time. Lorne began fly tying shortly after he made his first salmon fishing trip to the Miramichi in 1961: "We stayed at a cabin owned by Maurice Ingalls, famous for inventing the Butterfly. I caught my first salmon while on that trip and the fly was a Black Bear Green Butt."

The next year Lorne went to Newfoundland to fish Portland Creek. His guides were Riley House and David Caines, and Lorne has great praise for them: "Those fellows taught me how to salmon fish. They told me to fish close, often with only a rod-length of line, and to use small flies." Lorne was obviously a good pupil, as he caught five grilse in three days and remembers storing them under the moss until they left for home.

Lorne returned to Newfoundland every year until 1972. On that trip, he caught a record salmon: "It was in the pool below the lake," said Lorne. "That morning when I fished it I hooked six fish but only landed two; they were as wild as the dickens, fresh in from the sea. Later that evening I fished lower in the pool where several anglers had raised a big fish earlier." Lorne was fishing a #8 silver tip, and as he fished down to where the big fish lay, he hooked and landed a grilse. On his first pass over where the salmon lay, the fish rose but Lorne pulled the fly away from him. The fish took on the next swing and in the fight that followed, the fish led Lorne up and down the river and even into the lake. "Tom Caines was guiding an American and came up to where I was. He told me to let line out to form a belly in the current and he got out on a rock to gaff the fish. He missed the first as he was trying to gaff the fish in the back so he wouldn't harm the flesh, but the American sport gaffed him behind the pectoral fins and brought him ashore. He weighed thirty pounds." Lorne laughs when he remembers what happened next: "The guides told me that it was customary for the sport who caught the biggest fish to buy doubles for everyone, so a bunch of us walked out to the mouth of the river, where Manny had a kind of a club, and I sprang for the drinks. It cost me $100, and that was a lot of money in 1967."

Lorne was one of the early commercial fly tiers on Prince Edward Island and he continues to tie commercially today, supplying the Island Fly Shop with all their snelled trout flies. "I have an order for thirty-seven dozen this winter that I am working on. I used to tie a hundred dozen a year, but I've slowed down." Lorne says the Mosquito is always popular along with shrimp flies for trout out of the saltwater, and he likes to use the Montreal Streamer. Lorne continues to tie snelled trout flies, using eight-pond Maxima leader material for the snells.

Montreal Streamer

Tail:	Red hackle		Wing:	red squirrel
Body:	Claret wool		Hackle:	Claret, collared and tied
Rib:	Silver embossed tinsel			down

Brian Lewis

Brian was born in Alberton, Prince Edward Island, in 1933 and moved to Charlottetown with his family when he was eleven. He played baseball and hockey throughout the Maritimes before settling down in Charlottetown, and he was inducted into the Prince Edward Island Sports Hall of Fame and the Pictou County Sports Hall of Fame in Nova Scotia. He spent his career in sporting-goods sales, and this put him in contact with many anglers and fly tiers in the Maritimes.

Although Brian fished trout growing up, he was twenty-eight before he caught his first salmon, a grilse on the Miramichi. "We spent twenty seasons fishing on the Miramichi out of Jack Sullivan's camp," recalls Brian. "We had some great times."

Brian's interest in fly tying began on his first salmon fishing trip to the Miramichi: "I was fascinated by it, but the old-timers were very secretive about how they tied their flies. They wouldn't share anything with you."

Brian learned to tie flies from Frank Saunders, a self-taught tier. Brian hosted fly-tying clinics at the sporting-goods store where he worked and later taught classes himself. He was always happy to pass on what he knows to other tiers, going so far as to laugh, "I have no secrets."

Through his contacts in the sporting-good business, Brian became good friends with Leon Chandler of the Cortland Line Company: "I fished with Leon for eight years on the Margaree," recalls Brian. " We fished and stayed with Alex Libbus at his camp." Brian tied one hundred salmon flies for Leon Chandler when he went salmon fishing in Russia.

Brian remains actively involved in sports and is coaching several young ball players on the Island. He continues to tie flies and spends two weeks every fall salmon fishing on the Margaree and Baddeck Rivers in Cape Breton with his friend Dan Richard from Summerside.

Asked what makes a good taking fly, Brian laughs: "I was never a fish, so I don't know what to tell you. One thing I like to do is tie a small fly on a bigger hook. I'll tie a #8 fly on a #6 hook, for example." Brian also likes to tie most of his flies

General Practitioner

Hook: Salmon 2/0 to 6 single or double

Antennae: Sparse orange bucktail veiled by a tiny red-or-ange golden pheasant body feather

First half of body: Hot orange seal fur or yarn ribbed with oval gold tinsel and palmered with orange hackle

Back (from the centre of the hook): Golden pheasant tippet cut to a "V", cemented and tied flat over which is a golden pheasant body feather tied flat

Second half of body: Same as the first

Back (at the head of the hook): Golden pheasant body feather tied flat

Head: Red

very sparse: "On my Butterflies, for example, I seldom add a tail and only use a turn of hackle or none at all. The fly floats low in the water and you often hook the short takers."

Brian's favourite salmon flies for fall fishing are the General Practitioner, both red and black, and for summer he likes the Green Butt Butterfly or the Arbeau Killer, developed by Vaughn Arbeau in New Brunswick.

Buddy MacIntyre

Buddy was born and raised in Mount Stewart, Prince Edward Island. He attended the Halifax Police Academy and joined the Charlottetown Police Force in 1963, where he worked until 1971, when he went to work with the provincial government as a con- servation officer. Buddy began fishing as a boy and remembers using a one-piece bamboo pole and green twine as a line to fish for trout, using worms and a bottle cork for a bobber. Buddy has been fly fishing for forty years and made his first salmon fishing trip to Portland Creek in Newfoundland in 1970 with his friend Jack Chipman. As Buddy recalls, the water was very high on that first trip and he hooked only two fish. Their guide on that trip was Manny Caines, and Buddy remembers asking him which fly he should use. Manny replied, "Any fly you like, as long as it's a Thunder and Lightning."

Buddy took his first fly-tying class through the community schools in the early 1970s. The class was taught by Randy Dibble, and Buddy took to it immediately, enjoying the opportunity to tie flies the way he wanted. He later took courses on ty- ing traditional featherwing salmon flies from Ron Alcott. Buddy enjoys tying classic salmon flies and even converted one of his patterns, the Purple Passion, to a classic. He suggests beginning tiers consult Keith Fulsher and Charles Krom's book *Hair- wing Atlantic Salmon Flies* and Dick Stewart's *Universal Fly Tying Guide* for reference.

Buddy is a creative fly tier who enjoys experimenting with new materials as well as using different combinations of materials for his trout and salmon flies. He ties his Purple Passion fly with multi-coloured material he discovered in a fabric store.

His favourite fly is the Black Bear Green Butt. He likes to use black squirrel tail rather than the traditional black bear for the wing material.

> "'Trout' commonly was used at the turn of the century for all trout and char; scientific classification included many different species based on the wide variations in body shape, size, and colouration that exist in different geo- graphical regions. By the 1920s, the current classification was established, putting the trout into a half dozen species in the Genus Salmo and the Ge- nus Salvelinus. 'Char', its earliest use is from 1662, is taken from the Gaelic word caera (red, blood coloured) or caer (blood) in reference to these species' bright red bellies."
>
> Tor Fosnas, *In On The Pond* (1994)

Purple Passion

Tag:	Oval silver tinsel and purple floss		#071); front half: Black seal fur
Tail:	Golden pheasant crest	Rib:	Oval silver tinsel
Butt:	Black ostrich	Throat:	Soft purple hackle barbs
Body:	Rear half: Variegated My-lar thread (Gutterman's brand metallic thread	Wing:	Black squirrel
		Cheeks:	Jungle cock

Buddy likes his flies sparse: "They have better action in the water," he says. "A sparsely tied fly also sinks faster and gets down to the fish, while a heavily dressed one floats higher in the water column."

Buddy prefers to use partridge hooks for his salmon flies but he also likes the Medway line of hooks carried by Bryant Freeman at his shop, Escape Anglers, in Riverview, New Brunswick.

Buddy is also an avid trout angler and enjoys fishing streamers in the spring. The Grey Ghost is a favourite pattern, which he fishes on a sink tip line when the water is high and cold and the brook trout are just entering fresh water. Later, when he sees trout rolling on the surface, he switches to floating flies. One of his favourite flies for early trout is Shirley's Birthday, a pattern developed by Doug Wood and tied as a #10–12 wet fly. It has a silver body, grey fox wing, red tail and grizzly hackle. Buddy fishes trout throughout the spring, but shifts his focus to salmon fishing when the season starts.

A consummate road-tripper, for a few years Buddy was buying salmon licences for Newfoundland, Nova Scotia, New Brunswick, Quebec and Prince Edward Island. He's noticed differences between the provinces' flies: "On Newfoundland they like black flies, such as the Blue Charm and Thunder and Lightning. In the Maritimes flies with bright butts such as the Black Bear Green Butt seem to be more popular."

Buddy never goes fishing without his fly-tying kit: "That way I can tie up whatever local pattern the fish are taking, or if the fishing is slow, I can tie up something different that might work," he says. When he is away on a trip Buddy ties every evening. While he likes to use wet flies for salmon, Buddy is also partial to the Orange Bug.

Buddy taught fly-tying classes with his friend Tom Corcoran. He also worked with the Fly Fishing Federation when they were active on the Island. Although he doesn't tie commercially, his work is in demand at salmon dinners and other conservation events.

Dwayne Miller

Dwayne was born in Charlottetown in 1969 and has lived there all his life. He fished for trout as a boy and was introduced to fly fishing when he was twelve. He began tying flies in 1989, when a fly-tying friend of his gave him

All Points Bulletin

Hook:	Bartleet Supreme or Alec Jackson Spey	Rib:	Medium oval gold tinsel
Tag:	Flat silver tinsel	Throat:	Hot orange schlappen
Tail:	Golden pheasant tippet	Wing:	Three to four pracock swords followed by hot orange polar bear and topped with red squirrel
Body:	Kreinik metallic gold twisty, middle third peacock herl, front third same as first	Cheeks:	Jungle cock
		Head:	Hot orange

some pointers. Dwayne began selling his flies, and growing demand for his work led him to form his own fly-tying and guiding business in 1995. He provides guiding services for trout and salmon on the Morell and West rivers, two of Prince Edward Island's premier rivers for trout and salmon.

Dwayne mostly ties salmon flies these days, "a lot of bugs such as the Green Machine. Another popular bug is a white deerhair bug tied with brown hackle," he says.

His favourite pattern is one he developed, called the All Points Bulletin. "I first named it after a friend who saw a salmon tear through a pool and said, 'We should put an all points bulletin on that fish.' Later the meaning changed when my father-in-law Anthony Patrick Burton [APB] passed away from cancer in 2000. I first fished it on the West River here on the Island and it has been a good fly for me."

Dwayne likes to use jungle cock on his flies: "I think it adds a bit to the fly. I also like to tie my flies fairly full, not overly dressed but not too sparse either." Durability is important to Dwayne when he is tying his flies, and he uses head cement throughout the process to make tough flies. He ties most of his flies on the Medway hook sold by Escape Anglers in Riverview, New Brunswick, and he also likes the Partridge Bartleet hook for some of his patterns.

Dwayne is actively involved in sport-fish conservation through his involvement with the Prince Edward Island Salmon Association and the Central Queens Wildlife Association.

Steve Murphy

Steve was born in Summerside in 1969 and now lives in Borden with his family. He has fished since he was a boy, and his interest in fly fishing began about fifteen years ago. He obviously took to it: "I fish about a hundred days a year," he says. Ten years ago he began tying flies. He took a course through the community schools, but picked up most of what he knows on his own. He credits Poul Jorgenson's book on salmon flies as having had a big influence on his fly tying.

Steve began by tying hairwing salmon flies, but his interest in the history of the sport, and of fly tying, soon led to a desire to tie traditional featherwings as well. "Unfortunately I don't have a lot of time to tie them," he says.

Lester the Lobster

Hook:	Mustad 38941 #2–#10	Eyes:	30 lb mono melted
Thread:	Black Uni 8/0 and fluorescent red danville 6/0	Body:	Orange chenille, size depending on hook size
Feelers:	Four stripped orange hackle quills with a few strands of Krystal Flash	Hackle:	Orange
		Shellback:	Fluorescent fire orange laser wrap edged with red 6/0 thread
Feeler veiling:	Two or three golden pheasant breast feathers		

While Steve is an ardent salmon angler, he also fishes trout, and living on the Island he has excellent trout fishing available to him. He uses a lot of Stimulators, Adams, Caddis and Wulff flies. He says that Atlantic salmon are also fond of flies that many would consider to be traditional trout flies: "The black Woolly Worm and a silver-bodied Muddler are great flies for salmon on our rivers," Steve says. "Another good fly for both trout and salmon is Lester the Lobster. A lot of anglers swear by it for sea trout over here. The original calls for orange, but I also tie it in chartreuse for trout."

While Steve ties traditional wets, streamers and dry flies, he also likes to fish nymphs for trout. His woven body Bitch Creek nymph is a very neat and effective fly for trout. Steve favours a fairly sparse fly for most of his fishing.

Gordon Nicholson

Gordon was born in 1953 in Toronto but moved to Prince Edward Island at the age of four, when his parents returned to Upper Montague. He left to attend the Atlantic Police Academy in 1974. After graduation he joined the New Glasgow Police Department in Nova Scotia for five years. Later, Gordon and his wife decided to return to the Island, where he bought a feed mill that he continues to operate.

Gordon began fishing as a boy with an alder and a worm. He began fly fishing in 1981 when he met Mike Fitzgerald, who at that time ran Island Rods and Flies in Bonshaw. "I enjoyed fly fishing and that led to an interest in fly tying as well. I took fly-tying courses from Mike Fitzgerald, Tutty MacKinnon and Brian Lewis and that gave me a good start," he says.

Nick's Tan Seal Bug came about because Gordon wanted a bug that would float lower on the surface of the water: "I like to tie it in a variety of colours and fish it as a wet fly," Gordon says. "I mostly fish it on a sink tip line."

Gordon only carry eight or nine flies in a variety of sizes when he goes fishing, and he likes to put his flies in the water to see what they look like before he fishes

Nick's Tan Seal Bug

Tag: Flat gold tinsel
Butt: Green and red fluorescent yarn
Body: Tan seal fur
Hackle: Light ginger palmered forward over the body
Head: Orange thread

them. "The seal fur makes a very buggy looking fly when you look at it in water," he says.

Gordon had a bad fall when fishing a few years ago and finds it difficult to tie flies these days, although he is active in hockey and coaching. "I never tied commercially," he says, "only for myself and friends."

Stu Simpson

Stu was born in New Glasgow, Nova Scotia in 1937 and grew up there. He was introduced to sport fishing early in life by his grandfather and father, who were both avid anglers. Most of Stu's early fishing was for trout, and he made many fishing trips down to Guysborough County. After high school he began working for the Royal Bank, and one of his first transfers sent him to Charlottetown. Later transfers sent him to New Brunswick, where he began working in the insurance business, and eventually his work brought him to Summerside and finally to Charlottetown.

Stu's fly tying began after his first salmon fishing trip to Newfoundland, in the early 1970s. He purchased a dozen salmon flies from Charlottetown tier Tutty MacKinnon. As Stu recalls, the dozen flies didn't last long and he ended up buying some local flies. The flies he purchased weren't tied very well and came apart, so he figured that if he was going to continue as a salmon angler, he'd better learn how to tie his own.

That winter he attended a fly-tying course taught by MacKinnon and he has been tying ever since. As his interest and skill level increased, Stu began tying commercially for Canadian Tire in Charlottetown. Stu remembers tying 100 to 150 dozen flies every year, mostly trout patterns as there was not much demand for salmon flies. Although he continued to tie flies commercially for twenty years, he recognized that there was never much money in it: "The fly tying helped finance my fishing trips," laughs Stu. "I never made any money at it."

In 1987 Stu bought a fly-tying business, Island Rods and Flies, from Mike Fitzgerald. He operated the business until 2004, when he sold the retail end of the business to Harmen Boshuis, who operates it as Going Fishing. Stu continues to operate a custom rod-building business, Island Rods and Flies, where he builds handsome fly rods as well as massive deep-sea rods for sharks and tuna.

The most popular patterns for trout when Stu was in the business were the silver and standard Dark Montreal, Brown Hackle, tied with peacock herl body, White

Park Royal

Tag:	Flat gold tinsel	Rib:	Fine flat gold tinsel
Tail:	Golden pheasant crest	Wing:	Black squirrel
Butt:	Ostrich herl	Veil:	Pink hackle
Body:	Purple floss	Throat:	Yellow hackle

Miller and the male and female Mosquito. Saltwater streamers such as the Red Ibis and Royal Coachman were also big sellers.

Stu had to snell all his trout flies when he tied commercially, as Island anglers traditionally fished a two-fly cast. The most popular fly combination was a Dark Montreal on the point, combined with a female Mosquito on the dropper or bob.

The difference between a male and female mosquito is that "the female has a red band as a tag to imitate the blood sac," says Stu. Most of Stu's trout flies were tied on Mustad hooks, the 3399A and 3906B being the most popular.

Stu has continued to improve his fly-tying skills through classes, workshops and the study of books, especially Dick Stewart's *Universal Fly Tying Guide*. He attended Isaac Walton League fly-tying seminars in Ontario and when Ron Alcott came over to Charlottetown to conduct fly-tying workshops on classic salmon flies, Stu attended for six or seven years. However, materials for classic salmon flies are expensive and difficult to get, and he no longer ties classic flies, though he enjoyed the experience.

When he was in the retail business, Stu made up his own fly-tying kits, as he was disappointed with the ones available on the market. "I included a copy of Stewart's book with each of my kits," Stu says. Stu sold fly-tying books in his store, so he had a chance to review most of the books that are on the market. He credits Keith Fulsher and Charles Krom's *Hairwing Atlantic Salmon Flies* as one of the better books on tying salmon flies. Stu is a big fan of *SPAWNER* magazine: "For many years I tied every pattern profiled in *SPAWNER*, until I decided that I didn't need that many salmon flies," Stu laughs.

Stu began fly tying on a black Sunrise AA vice, and later switched to a Regal, which he continues to use for most of his fly tying. He also uses a Griffin as the jaws will accommodate the larger hooks he uses for mackerel flies.

When he began tying, Stu purchased his materials from Tutty MacKinnon, who ordered his materials from Veniards in England. Later, when he tied commercially, Stu purchased his fly-tying materials from Hook and Hackle in Alberta or Serge Boulard in Quebec. Although the bulk of his business was in trout flies, Stu also tied custom orders of salmon flies for anglers heading to New Brunswick, Nova Scotia or Newfoundland and Labrador.

The most popular streamers for sea trout on the Island are the Red Ibis and the Blockhouse, according to Stu. "The Red Ibis is tied with a silver body, no tail, and red goathair wing with a little bit of red hackle as a throat," he says. "The Blockhouse streamer was developed for fishing the tide water in Charlottetown

Harbour near the lighthouse, which is known locally as the Blockhouse. The fly has a yellow body and red wing with yellow hackle palmered through it."

Today Stu enjoys fishing small dry flies for Island trout. The parachute Adams is one of his favourites, and he made a fall trip last year to fish the Margaree, although much of his attention these days is directed at big-game fishing for tuna and shark.

Stu likes his flies sparse, and he tends to tie his salmon flies slightly low-water. He tailors his choice of hook to the type of fly he is tying—he favours Gamakatsu Salmon Fly Up Eye hooks or Partridge Bartleet Supremes for most his salmon flies, but will switch to a lighter hook for flies he fishes with the Portland Creek Hitch. He doesn't use doubles. His favourite salmon fly pattern is the Black Bear Green Butt. Among Stu's favourite self-developed flies is the Park Royal, named after his church, Park Royal United in Charlottetown. The fly came about one night when a friend of Stu noticed that the minister was wearing a colourful stole that Stu's friend thought would make a nice fly; he provided Stu with the colour combination and the Park Royal was the result. Stu fished the fly for the first time in Labrador. The first cast rose a fish and Stu took him on the second cast, a nice salmon. The fly has also been successful on the Margaree for fall fish.

"In the early part of the season the sea-trout, especially in tidal waters, prefer gaudy flies such as the red hackle and scarlet ibis, or a bright claret body with white wings. A distinction must be made in the size and colours of flies for use in the rough rapids, or in dark pools covered, as is often the case, with an inch or two of creamy or snow-white flocks of foam, also between those tied for the dark water of some streams which have their sources from lakes.… The same flies are not equally effective on dark days, or when the wind ripples the water and when the sun shines bright and clear.… Where the sportsman is compelled to confine himself to one fly for both bright and dark days, clear water or turgid, he could not do better than to select the Parmachene Belle, which is irresistible at almost all times to a feeding trout."

Arthur P. Silver,
Farm-Cottage, Camp and Canoe
in Maritime Canada
(1907)

Epilogue: The Future of Fly Tying in Atlantic Canada

There is no question that Atlantic Canada has a long and colourful history of fly tying. Fly tiers from this region were pioneers in the development of simple but effective flies for trout and salmon, and this tradition of innovative fly tying is alive and well today.

While salmon runs remain healthy in much of Newfoundland and Labrador, and on the Miramichi and Restigouche systems in New Brunswick, there is no question that runs have declined on some other rivers. Fortunately, conservation groups throughout Atlantic Canada are working hard to restore salmon and trout populations to their former greatness. In the meantime, anglers and fly tiers are concentrating on opportunities available to them. On Prince Edward Island brook trout, especially sea-run trout, continue to be popular with anglers and several fly patterns have been developed there to fish for them. In Nova Scotia, except for the Margaree River, most salmon fishing takes place during the fall on Northumberland Strait rivers, and fly tiers have crafted new patterns for fall fishing conditions. Nova Scotia tiers have also diversified their fishing and fly tying for sport fish that in the past were not as popular—native species such as American shad, striped bass and white and yellow perch, as well as introduced small-mouth bass and chain pickerel.

Many active programs throughout Atlantic Canada are working to ensure that the fly tying tradition will continue. The Atlantic Salmon Federation and its affiliates in the four Atlantic provinces use their Magic on the River program to introduce young anglers to fly fishing and fly tying. The Atlantic Salmon Museum in Doaktown has a similar program in place. Other opportunities exist through continuing education programs offered by community schools, recreation departments, sport-fishing organizations and fish and game clubs that offer introductory fly tying classes for new tiers. Frank Wilson, president of the Fredericton Fish and Game Club, says that the club has been offering fly-tying classes every winter since 1952, and every year the classes are full.

Other fly-tying opportunities can be found in less formal settings. Whether it is the Flies and Lies sessions held by the Sackville Rivers Association in Nova Scotia, or the fly tying socials organized by the Salmon Association for Eastern Newfoundland, there are fly-tying sessions held every winter throughout Atlantic Canada. During these sessions, experienced fly tiers volunteer their time to pass on their experience and knowledge to new tiers. Tiers such as Bas Vokey in St. John's and Dr. Harris Miller in Halifax have influenced several generations of fly tiers through their teaching.

A good measure of the level of interest in fly tying in Atlantic Canada is the success of the Dieppe Fly Tying Forum. Organized by the Moncton Fish and Game Association and the Dieppe Fly Tying Club, the event was first held in 2004. It featured fly-tying workshops and demonstrations by well-known tiers from the region. Last year the event attracted record crowds. In Nova Scotia, a Fly Tiers Association has been formed.

From my first days as a young angler up to the present time, fly tying has provided me with a great deal of enjoyment. The tying has always been fun, whether it is crafting flies for salmon or attempting to imitate local bait fish and insects for trout, and I have met many good friends through fly tying and fishing. I hope this book, like the organizations mentioned above, will help new fly tiers discover the pleasures of tying flies for fishing in the lakes and rivers of Atlantic Canada.

Fly-Tying Links

Atlantic Salmon Federation: www.asf.ca
Atlantic Salmon Museum: www.atlanticsalmonmuseum.com
Dieppe Fly Fishing Forum: www.flyfishingforum.globalsolutions.com
Fredericton Fish and Game: www.freewebs.com/fishandgame/index.htm
Margaree Salmon Museum:
museum.gov.ns/musdir/margareesalmonmuseum.htm
New Brunswick Fly Tyers: www.nbflytyers.com
New Brunswick Fishing: www.newbrunswickfishing.com
Nova Scotia Fishing: www.novascotiafishing.com
Nova Scotia Fly Tiers Association: riversedgeflyfishing@ns.sympatico.ca
Sackville Rivers Association: www.sackvillerivers.ns.ca
Saint Mary's River Museum:
museum.gov.ns/musdir/saintmarysriverassociation.htm
Salmonid Association for Eastern Newfoundland: www.saen.org
Salmon Preservation Association for the Waters of Newfoundland:
www.spawn1.ca
Salmon Anglers on Line: www.salmonanglersonline.com
Trout Nova Scotia: www.troutnovascotia.ca
Trout Unlimited: www.tucanada.org

Bibliography

Adney, Tappan. "Summer Days on the Miramichi." In F. Oppel. *Fishing in North America, 1876-1910.* Secaucus, NJ: Castle, 1986. Originally published in 1902.

Atlantic Salmon Journal. Various issues from 1957 to 2004.

Balfour, Harold. *Folk, Fish and Fun.* Suffolk: Terence Dallton, 1978.

Bates, Joseph D. Jr. *Atlantic Salmon Flies and Fishing.* Harrisburg, PA: Stackpole, 1970.

Bates, Joseph D. and Pamela Bates Richards. *Fishing Atlantic Salmon: The Flies and the Patterns.* Mechanicsburg, PA: Stackpole, 1996.

Brooks, Joe. *Complete Guide to Fishing Across North America.* New York: Outdoor Life Books, 1966.

Chaytor, A. H. *Letters to a Salmon Fisher's Sons.* London: John Murray, 1910.

Clarke, George Frederick. *Six Salmon Rivers and Another.* Fredericton, NB: Brunswick Press, 1962.

———. *The Song of the Reel.* Fredericton, NB: Brunswick Press, 1963.

Dashwood, Richard. *Chiploguorgan, or Life by the Campfire.* London: Simpkin Marshall, 1972.

Dowell, Jack. *The Look-Off Bear.* Toronto: McGraw-Hill Ryerson Limited, 1974.

Dunfield, R. W. *The Atlantic Salmon in the History of North America.* Ottawa: Department of Fisheries and Oceans, 1985.

Forrester, Frank. *Fish and Fishing of the United States and British Provinces of North America.* New York: W. A. Townsend Publisher, 1866.

Fosnas, Tor. *In on the Pond.* St. John's: Harry Cuff Publications, 1994.

Fulsher, Keith, and Charles Krom. *Hair-Wing Atlantic Salmon Flies.* Berlin, NH: FlyTyer, 1981

Greenaway, W. G. *The Way to Better Angling.* New York: McBride Co., 1954.

Grey, James T. 1987. *Handbook for the Margaree,* 3rd Edition. Earls Printing Company.

———. *Salmon Rivers of Cape Breton Island.* Earls Printing Company, 1984.

Grey, Zane. *Tales of Swordfish and Tuna.* New York: Harper & Brothers, 1927.

Hallock, Charles. *The Salmon Fisher.* New York: Harper & Brothers, 1890.

———. *The Fishing Tourist.* 1873; reprint, Derrydale Press, 1994.

Hardy, Campbell. *Sporting Adventures in the New World.* 2 vols. London: Hurst and Blackett, 1855.

Howley, James P. *The Beothucks or Red Indians.* Toronto: Coles Publishing, 1980. First published in 1915.

Karas, Nick. *Brook Trout.* New York: The Lyons Press, 1997

Kelson, George. *The Salmon Fly.* London: Messrs. Wyman and Sons, 1895.

Kennedy, W. R. *Sport, Travel and Adventure in Newfoundland and the West Indies.* London: William Black and Sons, 1885.

Leonard, J. Edson. *Flies.* A. S. Barnes and Company, 1950.

McCraith, Douglas. "By Dancing Stream." In Tor Fosnas, *In on the Pond.* St. John's: Harry Cuff Publications, 1994. Originally published in 1929.

McDonald, John. "Atlantic Salmon: Accounted King of Freshwater Fish." In *Fortune,* May 1948.

Netboy, Anthony. *The Atlantic Salmon: A Vanishing Species.* London: Faber and Faber, 1968.

Paine, Albert Bigelow. *The Tent Dwellers.* New York: Harper & Brothers, 1908.

Palmer, C. H. *The Salmon Rivers of Newfoundland.* Boston: Farrington Printing, 1928.

Parker, Mike. *Guides of the North Woods.* Halifax: Nimbus Publishing, 1990.

———. *Rivers of Yesterday.* Halifax: Nimbus Publishing, 1997.

Parker, H. E. (Ted). *Nova Scotia's Speckled Trout versus the Angling Novice.* Privately printed, 1973.

Rich, Len. *Newfoundland Salmon Flies and How to Tie Them.* Corner Brook, NF: Summerside Publications, n.d.

Russell, Jack. *Jill and I and the Salmon.* Boston: Little, Brown, 1951.

Sage, Dean, et al. "The Atlantic Salmon." In *Salmon and Trout: The American Sportsman's Library.* New York: MacMillan Publishers, 1902.

Schullery, Paul. *American Fly Fishing: A History.* New York: Nick Lyons Books, 1987.

Schwiebert, Ernest. *Art Flick's Master Fly Tying Guide.* New York: Crown Publishers, 1972.

SPAWNER. Various issues from 1979 to 2004.

Silver, Arthur P. *Farm-Cottage, Camp and Canoe in Maritime Canada.* London: George Routeledge & Sons, 1907.

Stewart, Dick. *Universal Fly Tying Guide.* Intervale, NH: Northland Press, 1979.

Thomas, Peter. *Lost Land of Moses: The Age of Discovery on New Brunswick's Salmon Rivers.* Fredericton, NB: Goose Lane Editions, 2001.

Underwood, John, and Ted Williams. *Fishing the Big Three.* New York: Simon and Schuster, 1982.

Webber, Ralph. *Salmon Summer.* Halifax: Oxford Street Press, 1983

Woods, Shirley. *Angling for Atlantic Salmon.* Goshen, CT: Anglers and Shooters Press, 1976.

Wulff, Lee. *The Atlantic Salmon.* Piscataway, NJ: Winchester Press, 1983.

Index of Flies

Note: Flies in colour insert are not indexed.

Index of Fly Tiers

Akroyd
Jerome Molloy

Albert's Surface Stonefly
Albert Jenkins

All Points Bulletin
Dwayne Miller

Big Intervale Blue
Len Rich

Bitch Creek Nymph
Steve Murphy

Black Ghost Butterfly
Art Eldershaw

Blockhouse
Eric Arsenault

Blue Mac
Allan MacLean

Bone Crusher
Doug Haney

Bow River Bugger
Larry Shortt

Bras d'Or Creeper
Rick MacDonald

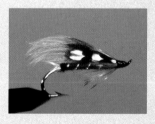

Brown Bomber
Joe Aucoin

Butterfly
Ray Buckland

Calftail Blue Charm
Paul Webb

Chimo
Don MacLean

Cosseboom
Eric Baylis

Cosseboom MacIntosh
Eric Jefferson

Crosby Special
Mike Crosby

Damsel Nymph
Harmen Boshuis

Danny Shrimp
Jack Ripley

Darbee's Spate Fly
Bill Carpan

Donnie's Black Fly
Don Ivany

Dunc's Smelt
Warren Duncan

Eastern Green Drake
Harmen Boshuis

Eclipse
Bob Baker

Elver Fly
Ian Gall

Eric's Bug
Eric Arsenault

Fred Forsythe Special
Leonard Forsythe

General Practitioner
Brian Lewis

**Ghost Streamer
Invincible**
Reg Baird

Gordie's Shrimp
Gordie MacKinnon

Green Cross
Tom Corcoran

Green Envy
Michael Brislain

Green Highlander
Don Hustins

Green Machine
Brian Sweeney

Guides Fly
Don MacLean

Hair Hackle Black Cosseboom
Frank Walsh

Handsome Dude
Cathy Colford

Hospitality
John Hart

Jock Scott Hairwing
Eric Jefferson

Killer Whiskers
Cathy Colford

Len Special
Leonard Forsythe

Lester the Lobster
Steve Murphy

Libbus Special
Alex Libbus

Lime Cosseboom
Earl Roberts

Little Codroy River Fly
John Sheppard

LT Special
Larry Tracy

MacIntosh
Danny MacIntosh

Maple Syrup Nymph
Tom Lee

McCoul Special
Jim McCoul

Medway Special
Lew Freeman

Meg's Special
Danny Bird

Mickey Finn
Damian Welsh

Mighty Bryson
Bill Bryson

Montreal Streamer
Lorne Kaiser

Mystery
Joe Aucoin

Neil's Green Machine
Neil Watson

Nepisiquit Gray
Doug Hanley

Nick's Tan Seal Hair Bug
Gordon Nicholson

North East Smelt
Jack Ripley

Orange Puppy
Reg Nichols

Orange River Shrimp
Marc Madore

Orange Shrimp Bug
Lorne Kaiser

Park Royal
Stu Simpson

Peacock Flasher
Keith Piercey

Peacock Olive Nymph
Ian Gall

Phantom
Eric Baylis

Pink Lady MacIntosh
Howard Ross

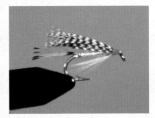

Pink Mystery
Bill Carpan

Pink Shad Fly
Larry Shortt

PM Hanging Emerger
Paul Marriner

Polar White
Bas Vokey

Purple Passion
Buddy MacIntyre

Rabbi
Bryant Freeman

RBM
Renate Bullock

Red Sac Fly
Don Hutchens

Reg's Hellgrammite
Reg Baird

Rocky's Upside-Down Fly

Earl Roberts

Ross Special
Howard Ross

Salmanier Special
Rick Maddigan

Saltwater Shrimp
Mike Fitzgerald

Same Thing Murray
Jacques Heroux

Shadow
Bob Baker

Silver Fox
Dave Fram

Smokey's Bug
Harold Ball

Specialist
Eric Baylis

Squirrel Tail
Don Barnes

Stimulator
Frank Walsh

Super Shrimp
Nick Martinello

Surface Stonefly
Brian Sweeney

**Thunder and
Lightning**
Don Hustins

Thunder Spey
Paul Webb

Undertaker
Frank Walsh

Waldo's Five Cent Fly
Waldo Hendsbee

**White Muddler
Minnow**
Bill Strople

Yellow Bucktail
Don Barnes